#MAKE

Chic

HAPPEN

this PLANNER BELONGS TO

_____

Follow Chic Online

@chicinfluencer @chicinfluencer Chic Influencer
@makechichappenplanner

Listen to Chic Online

Download the Make Chic Happen Podcast

Second Edition

Copyright © 2020 Chic Influencer
chicinfluencer.com

All rights reserved.

ISBN: 978-1-64713-102-9

Design by Margaret Cogswell
www.margaretcogswell.com

Table of Contents

THE STORY BEHIND THE PLANNER

Meet The Chaos Coordinators Helping You #makechichappen

We couldn't be more excited to help you grow your following and, more importantly, share your message with people who can connect with your story! And it's so nice to meet you here behind the scenes of your social media page. We know how much heart and time you put into your business, and we also know how frustrating it can be when you feel like you are doing all the right things, but it's not connecting with your audience. Our vision for creating this planner is to help you simplify your social strategy and clarify your specific marketing message through an easy-to-use social planner. We've included resources, content starters, weekly planning and reflection, brainstorming activities, and online trainings as well as a collaborative Facebook group.

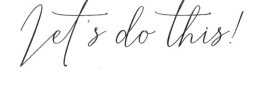

Let's do this!

Make sure you stay connected!
We want to see how you are using your planner.
Tag us **@chicinfluencer** using **#makechichappen**
and let us know what you think!

Please also join others using
#makechichappen planner on Facebook
facebook.com/groups/makechichappen/

Hey friends!

I am so excited to help you **#makechichappen**, but before we dive into rocking your social media marketing, I thought a somewhat proper introduction was in order! I am Katy, and I'm married to my college sweetheart (Mike). I have two boys (Nick and Dom), and I am a stage 4 blood cancer survivor. Before finding my passion for social media marketing, I spent about 9 years teaching 7th grade Reading. When I was on an extended maternity leave, I was diagnosed with cancer. During that time I started using my Instagram account and my Facebook account as a way to cope with the diagnosis and the battle through writing. The more I shared my writings, the more universal cancer became. Through writing, I felt more connected to

KATY URSTA

**CO-CREATOR OF
CHIC INFLUENCER**

others and less isolated through the struggles of cancer. In the past few years, my work has been featured on *The Today Show*, *Today Parents*, *Love What Matters*, *@ihadcancer*, *Her View From Home*, *For Every Mom*, and this year I published *The Back Pocket Prayer Journal* for women who, like me, wonder if they are "Jesus-ing wrong". Along with writing, I own a virtual health and wellness business and commit to helping my clients find a deeper motivation to fight for their own health. I am passionate about helping other entrepreneurs clarify and craft their unique message through the skill of social media storytelling.

But here's the deal, when I am not in the stands of my boys' hockey games, I am usually found folding the never-ending piles of laundry, looking for the matching sock, breaking up hockey fights, or (let's just be honest) with my hand buried in a bag of chocolate, asking my husband the question, "What do you want for dinner?" Come hang out with me over on Instagram **@katy_ursta** or on Facebook at **facebook.com/onefitfighter**

MELANIE MITRO

**CO-CREATOR OF
CHIC INFLUENCER**

Hey there, Melanie here! I am married to my husband, Matt, and I have two boys, Landon (11) and Bryce (9)! I live with my family live in Mars, PA.

I was the former Director of an Early Intervention Program that served clients from birth to age three. But after the birth of my first son, I left my full-time career to be a stay-at-home mom. I was introduced to network marketing when I was searching for a solution to get rid of the post-baby weight. In July of 2011, I launched my network marketing business with the vision of helping other mommas gain their bodies back after kids. I have been in the network marketing industry for the past eight years. I went from being a stay-at-home mom to the top distributor in the company in three years, creating a multi-seven figure income using social media as my primary source of marketing. I served on the Coach Advisory board for the company, and in 2018 I was given the CEO Award. I have a passion for teaching women how to strategically market their businesses through social media to drive results. I also love helping women develop systems, duplicate their success, and scale their businesses to give them freedom and purpose that fills their cup. I have spoken on stage for leadership conferences, annual summits, and local events.

When I'm not focusing on my business I'm either watching my two boys play basketball or baseball, or hanging out at home with the family snuggled up on the couch, watching a movie with a dirty martini in my hand. I have a tough love approach to business and I want nothing more than to see my tribe succeed. You can find more of my social media content @melaniemitro or on facebook.com/melaniemitro

GIRL, YOU MATTER, AND YOU ARE WELL ON YOUR WAY TO

#MAKING *Chic* HAPPEN

CONNECT WITH US

@CHICINFLUENCER
CHICINFLUENCER.COM
MAKE CHIC HAPPEN PODCAST

INTRODUCTION

Hi friend!

It's time to #makechichappen! Are you ready?

We see you over there, typing away in the early mornings, working on your dreams with a cup of coffee in hand and tired eyes that haven't yet peeled open completely.

We see you over there, working late into the night, after the kids have gone to bed, hoping the dishes have cleaned themselves and the laundry will just disappear.

We see you over there, building that dream while raising the kids, managing the house, rocking that full-time career, making time for the people who matter most in your life, and still managing to get the daily to-do list DONE.

You might not realize it but, girl, look at you: DOING THE DARN THING!

Gosh, we wish right now that we could pull up a chair beside you and tell you that you are doing an incredible job, that all those late night hours and early mornings are your success story in REAL TIME! The story you are writing and your decision to show up on your platform is making a real impact on the lives of others.

But since we can't do that, instead we will tell you that we are here on the other side of this planner, rooting for you, cheering for you, believing in you, and knowing that YOU can truly **#makechichappen.**

We know because we were once there, too.

We were exactly where you are, navigating the messy middle of "figuring it out," spending time watching YouTube videos and Googling everything about how to grow a social media following, early in the morning, late into the evening, and in the pockets of time that fit into the rest of our lives.

If we could boil down those seven years of learning social media into one big idea, it's this: *connection.* Everyone craves connection: being heard, being seen, and believing that someone has their back. It's important to connect to others who are walking through the same struggles that we are and connect with someone who's accomplished great things that we wish to achieve as well.

Connection is everything when it comes to cultivating community, converting followers into our clients, and, most importantly, leaving a lasting impact.

Even on social media where we are more connected than ever before, we can often feel isolated from the world around us. Ever feel like that? We can scroll without pause and catch ourselves going down a rabbit hole of comparison if we aren't careful.

Our vision is to simplify your social strategy and clarify your specific marketing message. This planner is designed to help you do just that.

The *Make Chic Happen Planner* is a personal guide to help you create a **Signature Style** of branding that helps you stand out in a noisy social media world and connect with those who need your message. .

We've laid this planner out into four sections. Before using the planner, we've created an overview for each section that will help you get the most out of your investment.

Sections of the Planner

#chicyoursocial
This section is a guide and resource to help you clarify your marketing strategy, create your ideal audience, and convert your prospects into raving clients.

#chicgoals
This section is a working document to help you outline your big ideas with the small, more attainable mile markers that will directly connect to the big wins.

#chicitup
This section is additional resources that we've created to help you build a memorable and unique brand.

#makechichappen
This section is your weekly planner which contains 52 to weeks for you to brainstorm

your strategy for the week while reflecting on brand growth, messaging, and overall conversion. Here you will reflect on your marketing for the week, break down your weekly stats, analyze your brand messaging, and clarify your messaging for the week ahead.

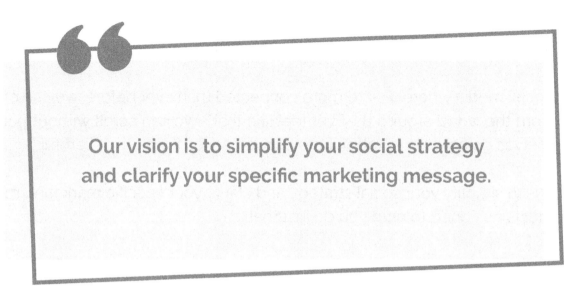

Our vision is to simplify your social strategy and clarify your specific marketing message.

#Chic YOUR SOCIAL

#CHICYOURSOCIAL

Chic your social in three easy steps:
1. *Know and Speak to Your Ideal Followers*
2. *Create Engaging Content*
3. *Convert Your Followers into Consumers*

Katy here! Before I discovered online marketing, I was a 7th grade Reading teacher. I spent years creating lesson plans that would connect students to the universal struggles of characters across a variety of genres. I knew that if my students felt connected to the characters, they were sold on the story. Connection, when it comes to any type of marketing, is the key to converting potential followers into lifelong believers.

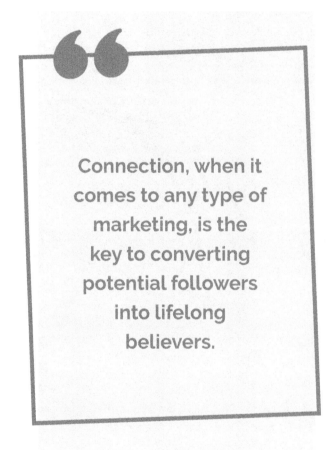

Connection, when it comes to any type of marketing, is the key to converting potential followers into lifelong believers.

As Melanie and I started focusing on our VISION for the **#makechichappen** planner, we realized that we had to include our *Signature Style* of marketing.

Signature Style (def.)
An individual's unique marketing spin on the product or service they offer that sets them apart from the competition.

The **Signature Style** creates genuine and authentic connection, establishes trust through consistency and credibility, and provides a unique perspective of the service or the product to the audience.

Creating the **Signature Style** starts with understanding your current personal social media marketing strategy. On the next page, check off each box that you CONFIDENTLY believe describes your current social media.

QUIZ

I believe in the products and services I offer.

I confidently share content that feels "unposed" and real.

I authentically engage with my audience and it never feels "salesy."

People often share my content because of the value I add.

I don't scramble to post. I purposefully create content that is directly connected to my marketing plan.

I create an opportunity for my followers to engage with my content but they are also engaging with one another.

I see my platform as an online community where I can serve my audience.

I genuinely enjoy conversing with the people who show up on my social platforms.

My audience relates to my content; it is relevant to them.

I LISTEN to my audience and share content that they request.

I collaborate with other influencers outside of my industry.

My audience trusts my advice.

I convert followers into clients through natural conversation and excitement for what I have to offer.

I am growing a loyal following that creates a constant pipeline for invitations, follow ups, and testimonials.

TOTAL:

If you scored 1-4 that means that we have some work to do with your brand.
If you scored 5-9 that means you are on your way to growing a strong, unique and authentic brand.
If you scored 10-14 that means that you have a solid brand and the goal is to continue creating content in a way that attracts your ideal target consumer.

> Trust, connection, and community take time to foster and grow.

So, how did you do? Do you feel like you're already **#makingchichappen** or could you shake up your chic a little bit? Let's be honest, NO ONE checks off all the boxes, and that's ok! The goal of your marketing is to focus on progress over perfection. Pay attention to what your audience LOVES and what you can do to create more engagement!

This checklist is EXACTLY why we've created the *Signature Style*. Marketing is meant to be fun. Happy clients are created when they feel they are being served before they've even reached for their wallets. Finding space on the loud platforms we call Instagram and Facebook is not hard to do, but online marketers RARELY take the time to do it.

WHY? Because trust, connection, and community take time to foster and grow. Too often we want to rush the sale instead of slowing down enough to ASK what our followers REALLY want from us. What people really want has little to do with the actual products and much more to do with the feelings associated with them. You, my friend, are creating a feeling through your *Signature Style*. So are you ready to dig in?

> Signature Style (def.)
> An individual's unique marketing spin on the product or service they offer that sets them apart from the competition.

1. KNOW AND SPEAK TO YOUR IDEAL AUDIENCE

One of the biggest things we see online marketers struggle with is creating authentic connections. Often we hear:

"Who do I invite?"
"How do I not come off as salesy?"
"How can I gain more followers?"
"How can I start being seen more?"

It doesn't matter how many people you have following you if you're not authentically connecting with your audience. The goal is to create content that feels inviting. I see the word invite not just as one simple action but as the emotion we create on our feed. I want to make people "feel" invited so I don't have to cross my fingers and hope that a stranger will say yes.

Pro Tip: head over to the #chicitup section because we have left you some of our top podcast episodes for creating great content.

People naturally look for others to connect with, so the first questions I encourage other business owners to ask is, "Am I showing up for others or am I simply showing up to check off a box? And, "Am I showing up to sell a product or am I showing up to serve my audience?" Creating captions that include the audience shift the focus from you (the writer) to them (the audience). For example, when you are sharing the products or the services you are selling, do you create a caption that gives the feeling of "look at me" or a feeling of "look at what can be?"

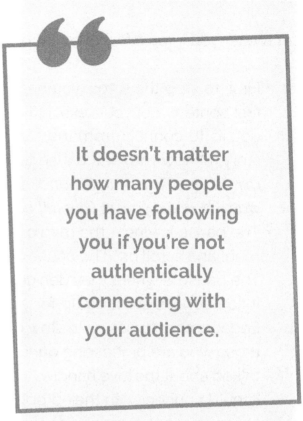

> It doesn't matter how many people you have following you if you're not authentically connecting with your audience.

Does your content shout to the audience "Good for you!" or does it sound like, "Ok, maybe I can do this, too." Inspire others to want to do what you do rather than just *liking* what you do. Focus on serving! What you share isn't about you, it's about what you can do for others.

2. CREATE ENGAGING CONTENT

We want the audience to do something or think something immediately with a post. Let's be real, as marketers, social media can feel like you're stuck in a traffic jam on I-95 looking for the opportunity to find the nearest exit! Even if the back roads take a little longer, you can rest assured that it's better than staying stuck! Am I right!?! I mean, standing out means that we sometimes have to slow down, pay attention to the signs and occasionally reroute!

I want to let you in on a little secret. If you want to be seen, get out of traffic! Stop trying to please the masses, and make your message meaningful to the people that you truly want to connect with.

Want a big business? Focus on serving small!

Let me let you in on a few of my go-to, tried and true tips:

- First, to stop the scroll, you need a captivating image with a matching tagline (the first sentence of your text). I love sharing a relatable story starter with just enough details to connect from the start! If my followers can visualize themselves in my story, I know they will pause to read more! For example, *"I stood in the bathroom mirror, pinching my love handles with tears in my eyes and all I could think to myself was ... how did you let yourself go?"*
- The pause is where the magic happens because it's the bridge between engagement and scroll on. The pause creates the connection, and connection builds trust. The pause is where they decide to click "see more" and read the entire caption.
- If someone is showing up for you, you must let them know that you are listening. Engagement forces us to slow down, to think about our words, and to interact with those who are processing our content. For example, in the example above where I talked about the love handles, I go on to describe how they might be feeling so that I could connect with their problem.
- I keep my sentences short using italics, ellipses, or even emojis to keep my followers interested. I pay attention to small details that connect me to them whether that's the music I listen to, the way I mother my kids, or some of my childhood pop culture memories.
- You want to show people that when they comment you are going to be there to respond. This creates personal connection between you and the individual follower (remember we are speaking to individuals, not masses). It is the foundation of how relationships are built. When you cultivate conversation, think about it as a drip of dopamine: you want to come back for more. That reinforces the followers' commenting behavior and increases the likelihood that they will interact the next time you post. It's not just a post anymore; it's an opportunity to cultivate community. When I post I make sure to stick around for a little while and engage with people as they're commenting. This will boost your engagement on the post and your platform will recognize this content as "of value" and show it to more people.
- Then, take the next steps. If someone likes, comments, or watches, this is what I call eye contact. If someone is kind enough to check you out, reciprocate! Engage with

their account. Take note of their life and look for opportunities to connect on their page. Bottom line, conversation—authentic, light and meaningful conversation—is what makes conversion FUN!

3. CONVERT YOUR FOLLOWERS INTO CONSUMERS

Conversion is simplified when you have common ground. It will never feel icky when you FEEL as though you've been serving people long before you've made an offer. I find that my audience gets excited to hear about products, experiences, services, or joining my team after they've been engaging with me, getting to know me, and cultivating a social connection! It's kind of like dating, isn't it? Over time, trust is built around common connections. TRUTHBOMB: TRUST TAKES TIME! If you're focused on selling instead of serving, you won't convert followers into clients. As an influencer, it's our responsibility to make sure we are sharing our products and services in a way that is authentic to our beliefs. You build trust over time with each post that you create. Every story you tell bridges the gap between who you are and how you can serve your audience. Remember, a successful post isn't determined by a set number of likes or comments, it's when the post creates meaningful conversation. *For more information on how to create trust visit https://chicinfluencer.com/free-resources*

If someone is showing up for you, you must let them know that you are listening.

Before you post, ask yourself a few general questions:
- What kind of reaction do I want? Action or thinking? Do I want my audience to do something immediately with the post, or do I want them to sit with my words? *Note: never underestimate a call to think post. This creates trust in a comeback audience.
- What do I want them to do with this post? Drop an emoji, help me, give me advice?
- Am I creating community?
- Are these words I'd actually use in real life?
- If I read my post out loud to myself or my best friend, would my words match my personality? For example, I use words like "dude", "do you", "boo", and "hey yinz guys"…
- Does my image match my content? For example, if I am talking about my life as a boy mom, or something my husband said, am I including them in the image so my

audience can create a clearer picture?

For more tips, head to https://chicinfluencer.com/free-resources

Your Signature Style

The **Signature Style** is the unique marketing spin on the product or service you offer that sets you apart from the competition. It is essential to clarify your message, audience, and online community in order to create a thriving social media strategy. We have broken your brand down into three distinct categories that are required for you to grow your ideal audience.

The three categories are:
1. *Connection*
2. *Belief*
3. *Your Unique Sharing Proposition*

If you have two categories but not the third you will be missing a key part of the **Signature Style**. You need all three categories to have an impactful brand. Let's break this down.

CONNECTION

Personality, visual appeal, and community create the outer ring of the **Signature Style** called connection. First, personality is who you are as an individual. Are you someone who loves to laugh and make others laugh? Are you someone of faith? Do you use cuss words in your everyday life? Is your health and nutrition a priority? If you want to get clarity on your personality, just ask your best friend and/or loved ones to describe the unique characteristics that make you, YOU! Then ask yourself, "Do those characteristics shine through in my social media content? Would my friends read my posts and say, 'Yup, that is Melanie!!'" If the answer is no, then we have some work to do in this category.

The second factor that creates connection is community. We define community as the people who are going to be commenting and interacting with one another on your posts. A simple way to begin fostering community on your social media is to create content that encourages others to engage together in a thread you've begun. So, for example, if you are an individual who homeschools their kids, is your community homeschooling moms who connect and talk to one another in the comments?

For me (Melanie), my audience consists of many business owners. I know when I post business advice, tips, strategies, or how "I built this", my community is going to respond.

If you don't know WHAT your community is right now, don't stress! It took both Katy and me time to get our community refined. Once you figure it out, trust me: it is incredible to watch your followers connect through your content.

For more tips, head to https://chicinfluencer.com/free-resources

The third area is the visual appeal. Visual appeal is the look and feel of your feed.
- Do you have a color scheme you follow?
- Do you have pops of color?
- Do you have white quotes every 3rd photo?
- Do you gravitate towards black and white?

You do not have to be super formal and professional on your page if that is not your brand! Ask yourself, "When people click onto my account, what do I want the first experience to be like?"

Note: These are not things you MUST do, these are suggestions to help you think about what you want your social to look like.

I am constantly opening up my social media, taking a step back, and asking myself if I like the look and feel of the visual content I am creating. I am refining and improving my visual appeal so that I am always captivating my audience. It is also important that you are consistently showing up on social. Consistency is defined by what you feel you can commit to on a regular basis. I am not going to tell you that you need to commit to a certain number of posts per day. I will tell you that consistency is going to be the differentiator between you and others in your social media growth and engagement.

BELIEF
Belief is defined as what you have to offer as well as the belief you have in yourself creates the energy that draws people to your brand.

I start by asking myself a few key questions about my own belief systems.
- Do you believe that YOU are the best person for the job that you are doing?
- Do you believe that you are destined for success?
- Do you see where you want to be?
- Can you visualize your dreams becoming reality and how you will celebrate that victory?!
- Do you believe in your ability to figure out all of the steps along the way?

Belief in yourself is the CORE of your success. This is the part of the *Signature Style* that requires daily heart work. Do you currently carve out time every day for personal development? If not, pull out your calendar and let's make it a priority every single day.

Secondly, do you believe in the product and/or services you offer? If the answer is no, then that is a HUGE roadblock. In order to effectively promote a product, service, or business, you have to believe that your product can change someone's life for the better. Confidence in what I offer came with practice, educating myself, and my own testimonial. You cannot effectively sell what you do not believe in.

YOUR UNIQUE SHARING PROPOSITION

Your unique sharing proposition is how you do what you do in just a slightly different way that makes people stop, lean in, and get curious. Outside of your marketing industry, how are you seen by others?

This is the part of your brand where you show how you do business just a tad differently than the competition.

For example, if you are a makeup consultant, do you serve women over forty? Do you share day and night looks? Do you use drugstore makeup and show people how to get glam on a budget, or are you all about the high-end products?

You have a unique spin and way that you do WHAT YOU DO. This separates you from the others who offer a similar product or service. It comes down to WHY you do the work you do. I will caution you that comparing and creeping on other people in your industry is going to make you feel like a carbon copy and not an original. Following other people in your industry also robs you of your own creativity and can cause writer's block. Bottom line ... YOU DO YOU, BOO!

It is in this third section, your unique sharing proposition, where you can ask people to interact, you can direct them to inquire about your services, and you have earned the right and the trust with your followers to ask for the sale. This is where your SWEET spot of sales is! Remember, if it feels icky, it's because you aren't using the *Signature Style*. Each post we create provides a call to act (what do we want our followers to do—reach out, watch our stories, head to a link in the bio, swipe to see more, comment, give feedback, etc.) or a call to think (a post that creates conversation or encourages connection). This type of post creates a comeback audience because we are serving them with a feeling.

Once you are implementing all three categories you'll begin to see that your business is thriving and not just surviving! This is where you feel your JOY meter rising because you are serving your IDEAL audience, and it just feels RIGHT!!!

Alright it is your turn! *We have an entire video on your Signature Style if you check out our online portal at https://chicinfluencer.com/free-resources.*

We've included a blank signature plan on the next page for you to brainstorm essentials of creating that know, like, and trust factor. We encourage you to take time to really identify what your unique sharing proposition is so that you can serve your audience well. Remember, the more consistent you are with creating connection, the more your belief will grow. Your audience will become attracted to the confidence you have for uniquely showing how you do business differently! Let's brainstorm!

CONNECTION

BELIEF

YOUR UNIQUE SHARING PROPOSITION

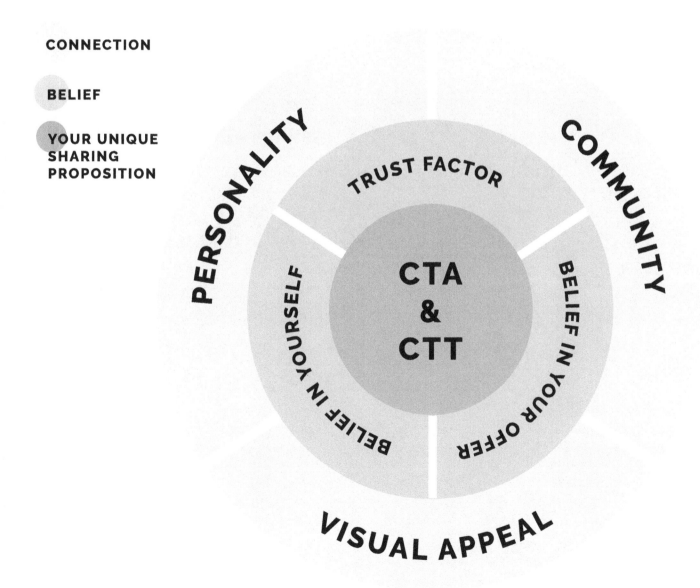

my signature plan

CONNECTION

BELIEF

YOUR UNIQUE SHARING PROPOSITION

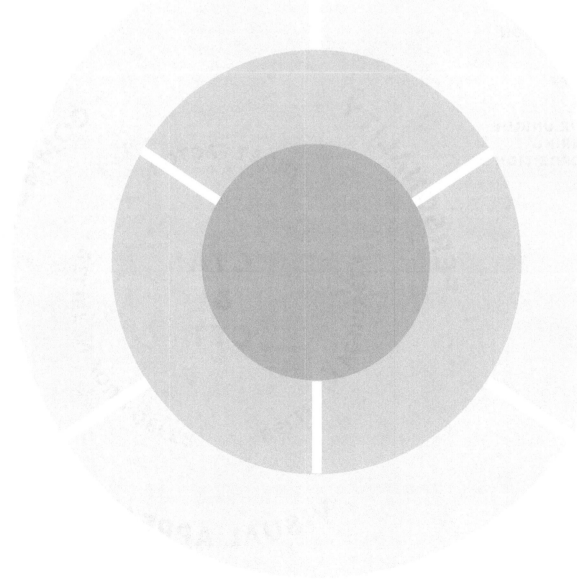

#Chic
GOALS

Setting clear and defined goals is ESSENTIAL when it comes to creating a solid strategy for your social media. Every single successful business owner has the ability to connect his/her income and growth goals to their marketing strategy. I (Melanie) sometimes feel like we spend all this time setting our business goals and then we set separate social media goals, then the two areas don't speak to each other which is a huge problem. Your social media content and your goals should be directly related to your bottom line. After all, the reason you are creating social media content is to grow your know, like, and trust factor so that you can create more sales, RIGHT?!

In this section, we are going to ensure that our social media content is directly related to our business goals. There will be no more throwing spaghetti at the wall to see what sticks. Our social media has a purpose, whether it's connection or call to action, there is always a point to what we are putting out there. So let's dig into goal setting.

There are two parts to goal setting. You have the end goal and then you have the smaller goals that are required to achieve in order to get to the end goal. We call the smaller goals "mile markers". One of our gifts is being able to see the big picture of the end goal and break that down into smaller, more manageable quarterly, monthly, weekly, and daily activities. I believe that in order to effectively communicate your message you have to be clear on the objective and the end goal you are working towards.

When it comes to creating content, I used to cross my fingers, hoping my message would stick for someone. Friend, hope is NOT a strategy.

When it comes to creating content, we want to make sure it aligns to our business goals. I (Katy) used to cross my fingers, hoping my message would stick for someone. Friend, hope is NOT a strategy. Think of it like this, you are on the lookout for a new pair of jeans. You know the kind: they hit your curves in all the right places, stretch just enough when you overindulge, and are totally within budget. You know exactly what you are looking for, the cut, the color, the overall feel, and you know exactly how those jeans are going to look! You have visualized those bad boys so clearly that when you head over to the mall, you refuse to settle for anything less.

You are the intentional shopper with an end goal in mind. You are not distracted by the sweaters in aisle 7 or the clearance rack. Girl, you are on a mission to get #demjeans! In your business using the Chic **Signature Style** activity, you will know exactly what "jeans" are best for your audience. You know how to serve them well, and aren't distracted by discounts, off brands, or "less than the best" feel. You are intentional with you messaging to get an audience that is "just the right fit" for your messaging.

CHIC YOUR YEAR

So let's **#makechichappen!** You have to start with the big picture before you can just jump into creating content. First, ask yourself, what is your big goal for the next twelve months? Where do you want to be twelve months from now? What kind of business do you want to have? What does your business look like? What products or services are you delivering to your clients? How many customers do you want to have? How much income are you earning? How many subscribers do you have on your email list? How many people are a part of your community? Is there a certain number of collaborations you want to do this year? How big is your team? Let's just brain dump all of your thoughts onto a sheet of paper.

This is where you have to allow yourself to dream big and get a little uncomfortable with what you want your social media to look like one year from today. With your social media, what do you want to accomplish in the next twelve months? Pro tip: Don't get stuck in knowing EXACTLY where you want to be at the end of the year. When I do the yearly goals, it is a bit of a leap of faith and sometimes a stab in the dark. I look at the previous year and estimate potential growth. I set an income goal that is over and above the year before. I set an income goal that challenges me, but isn't completely unrealistic. There is nothing wrong with tweaking goals during the year if things aren't going as planned. But, when we don't set goals at all because we are afraid we won't reach them, that is where the problem lies. So, don't overthink this section, let's set some goals. Below, I've given you a few examples. Please note how each goal is SMART. Writing a smart goal means that it is specific, measurable, attainable, realistic and timely. EXAMPLES MIGHT INCLUDE:

12 MONTH GOALS:

1. I will make $100k in sales from online courses by December 31, 2021.

2. I will have 5,000 emails on my email list by December 31, 2021.

12 MONTH GOALS CONTINUED:

3. I will advance my business to (insert rank) by December 31, 2021.

4. I will do 1 collaboration per month with complimentary companies to expand

reach.

Now it's your turn! Remember to make your goals specific, measurable, and realistic, yet challenging and timely! You don't have to have all four goals, but make sure these are goals you feel will help you grow in the direction you envision your business going.

12 MONTH GOALS:

1.

2.

3.

4.

The next step is to divide each goal into 4 quarters.

NOTE, it does not matter if you start this planner in July or in January. The goal is to start now and not wait until a fresh week, month, or year.

In the next four months, what will you accomplish? This requires baseline data. Take a look at your current business and ask yourself where you are today and what is realistic for you to accomplish in the next four months.

For example, if you want to grow your email list to 5K in the next year, what is your current number of subscribers? Subtract your current subscribers from the goal of 5,000. If you divide that number by 12, then you have your monthly growth goal for your email list.

Example, I have 1,500 subscribers.
5,000-1,500= 3,500
3,500/12= 291 .6 emails per month.

Does that feel doable? If so, then you have set a goal that is doable yet challenging.

By setting this monthly goal you can create a list of ways to always be increasing your email list. That might translate into a freemium that you create and promote on social media. You could run an ad to that freemium and more!

If your goal is to grow your email list, then you will always be thinking of ways to drive people back to your list.

We will be going over how to create more strategies to reach your goals in the next section too.

> **If you want intentional social media growth you have to be focused on activities that are going to drive that bottom line.**

LET'S TAKE ACTION!

So now it's your turn. Write out your goals for the next twelve months, break them down, and then chart out your quarterly game plan.

YEARLY GOALS:
Goal 1: I will make $100k in sales from online courses by December 31, 2021.
Baseline: I have not created any courses yet.

Goal 2. I will have 5,000 emails on my email list by December 31, 2021.
Baseline: I have 1,500 email subscribers to date.

Goal 3. I will advance my business to (insert rank) by December 31, 2021.
Baseline: I am currently at _____ rank.

Goal 4. I will do 1 collaboration per month with complimentary companies to expand reach.
Baseline: I've done 6 collaborations in 2020.

QUARTER 1	QUARTER 2	QUARTER 3	QUARTER 4
Goal 1 make $25k through online courses	Goal 1 make $25k through online courses	Goal 1 make $25k through online courses	Goal 1 make $25k through online courses
Goal 2 875 emails per quarter	Goal 2 875 emails per quarter	Goal 2 875 emails per quarter	Goal 2 875 emails per quarter
Goal 3 Advance my business to the next rank	Goal 3 Advance my business to the next rank	Goal 3 Advance my business to the next rank	Goal 3 Advance my business to the next rank
Goal 4 3 collaborations each quarter	Goal 4 3 collaborations each quarter	Goal 4 3 collaborations each quarter	Goal 4 3 collaborations each quarter

QUARTER 1	QUARTER 2	QUARTER 3	QUARTER 4

CHIC YOUR PLAN

We have to start thinking of all the ways that we can reach the goals we've set for ourselves. This is why the planner is so important. We can create content that drives your end goal. Every week in your planner you are going to track your progress towards your goal, what were your wins, what were your challenges, and how you will address them in the next week.

We are going to walk you through a month of planning and how we use the planner to layout our content (see page 34-35 for an example calendar).

Every month we ask ourselves a series of questions:
- What are some of the known obstacles we will face (vacations, holidays, back to school, trends of consumers based on market research)?
- Do I have any deadlines this month?
- Are there any new product launches, sales, or promotions I want to run?
- How will I get ahead and plan for these challenges so my business maintains steady growth?

Example: We are writing this planner in August and we are in the thick of back-to-school. That is a HUGE hurdle for our market (known obstacle). Most working mommas are running around like chickens with their heads cut off: school clothes shopping, open houses, teacher/parent orientation, fall sports, and still maintaining the house plus business tasks.

We know that during August women are a little more strapped for cash (known obstacle) and are less likely to invest in a product that is going to require sacrifice or a new routine. We have to leverage that in our marketing plan. For example, we are going to focus on handling objections, giving women advice for how to plan for the craziness of the month and tailor our services in a way that speaks to the very busy and cash-strapped woman. Make sense?

We know that if we offer a product or service, we need to capitalize on the first half of August (this is how I get ahead of the challenges) so that we're not scrambling during the Labor Day holiday to close sales or feel like we're pushing people towards our own agenda. Everything in the second half of the month should be gravy, baby! If the end of the month is a deadline for you, make sure you incorporate that into your planning.

Next, we pull out the blank monthly calendar and we start writing our marketing game plan.

Pro Tip: Write the launch date for whatever product or service you are promoting. What is the last possible day people can purchase? Then, you work backwards. Count 10-14 days before the goal date, that is the FIRST day you will begin marketing your promotion.

The reason we take 10-14 days to promote a product is because our audience needs to hear the message multiple times before they commit. Remember, it's normal for a very small amount of your following to see your content, so the more you relay a message, the higher the likelihood that your following will convert to clients.

Now we create our ideas for marketing our promotion. We start by asking ourselves questions like:
  • What about that product is unique or different?
  • Who is this product/service for?
  • Why should people buy it from you and not someone else?
  • Why are you the best person for the job?
  • What is your unique angle and spin on what you do?
  • What do people ask you for advice about over and over?
  • What questions will people have about what you are offering?

We think about our market and their potential objections, their possible questions, and what our unique spin on service is. The more clearly we can answer these questions, the higher the likelihood that our audience will connect with our promotion.

This is your brainstorming session. Get all of your ideas out on paper so you can begin to make sense of it all.

As you look at this sheet of paper you can begin to organize into your weekly plan. Take the messy, big ideas you've brainstormed and create a weekly marketing layout.

Pro Tip: Keep your marketing focus on ONE major marketing theme weekly. It's important to remember that your audience won't likely see ALL of your content, so you don't want to confuse them with multiple messages. Occasionally it's ok to market something small, like a pop up sale or launch that you know will quickly sell out.

CUSTOMER LOVE

I love all the great information provided in the book to teach you authenticity! -Makayla Kane

I struggled with planning my social media content. This planner has provided everything I needed to guide me in planning and creating content that is meaningful and appropriate for my target market! This has been a game changer for my business :) - Michelle

I love it. Especially the reflection part!!! A business can't grow without reflection of what customers like and don't like. - Gina Yost Johnston

I use it everyday for personal and business! - Teresa

I love my planner! It not only helps keep me organized and plan my content for the week, it allows me to see where I may need to make some changes! With so many distractions, it's a must! - Yanik Fenton

PURCHASED! LOVE it! And beyond the planner the FREE! yep FREE...help, guidance and trainings on how to use it and not let it collect dust are invaluable! - Katie McClave

month:

August

marketing focus:

*chic your gram audits

*community membership

*podcast growth

MONDAY	TUESDAY	WEDNESDAY
3	(4) start chic gram marketing	5
10	(11) training LIVE on #4hashmethod	12
17	market 18 community open enrollment [Q&A]	19
24	25	26
31	community 1 closes enrollment (50)	

MONTHLY GOALS: sign 10 new chic your gram members, enroll 50 new community members

THURSDAY	FRIDAY	SATURDAY	SUNDAY
		1	2
		add value days - - - - - - - - - - - - →	
podcast 6	7	8	9
- →			
podcast 13	(14) chic gram spots filled due date (10)	15 add value days	16
podcast 20	21	22	23
- →			
podcast 27	28	29	30
- →			

Now that we have BIG goals set, we have the BIG vision of where we want to go, and now we're really ready to start doing the work! At full disclosure, numbers and stats have never been my (Katy's) jam. In fact, part of me still twitches when I think of Mike and his weekly excel budget sheets. But when it comes to understanding the trends in my business, numbers and stats are like unlocking the great algorithm mystery.

CONNECTION drives all content choices. I use my stats to help me decide how to serve my audience. Melanie and I have spent weeks using this section of the planner to make sure that we are helping you **#makechichappen**.

This section of the tracker has 3 main categories:

1. *Reflect & Refine*
2. *My Income Producing Activity Tracker*
3. *Weekly Marketing Plan*

Reflect & Refine

In order to get where you want to go, you have to embrace and learn from where you've been. Through this section, each week you will complete an inventory of your wins, your plot twists, and "whys". Melanie and I have learned to lean into the reactions and feedback of our audience by evaluating weekly how our content is received. It's an opportunity to grow and become more effective at serving our audience! This section also allows us to track our business results so we can make sure our media marketing is making an impact on the bottom line!

Tracking Your Social Media Stats

Analyzing our weekly Instagram and Facebook trends is an important part of our growth because it gives us indisputable evidence about what our audience and new followers want to see, how well we are serving, and if it's leading to conversion. As Melanie says, when we are intentional about our content, we don't just throw spaghetti at the wall, hoping something will stick. We know what our audience wants and we use that feedback to help us create the next week's social media marketing plan.

I will say it again. "Tracking reveals trends, trends reveal the truth, and the truth will set you free!"

Can I get an amen? Goodbye guesswork; hello strategic media growth!

Tracking results
Before setting new goals, we want to reflect on our habits from the previous week. We don't want to focus solely on the outcome, but also on our output (our efforts.) Both Melanie and I feel as though it takes a consistent 7-10 days to effectively market an idea, a product, a service, or an experience for people to begin to notice. And if we aren't seeing an impact on the bottom line, we might need to adjust our marketing.

Three areas are noted for tracking results:
- How many invitations did I send?
- How much income did I earn?
- How many enrollments did I have?

It's worth noting that INVITATIONS happen through conversation. When you are tracking your invitations, do not put an emphasis on the number of posts you do that call people to respond, but the actual conversations you have with an individual.

When it comes to tracking your income, focus on income you produce through the use of social media. We recommend focusing on commissions generated through social media efforts. When it comes to enrollments, this should be specific to your current marketing efforts, whether you are focusing on enrollment into your VIP Launch Page, your team, your bootcamp, your email list, your new course, or even a product test group. Enrollment is a specific number of people who've opted in because of your efforts!

Tracking your wins & plot twists for the weeks
While analyzing the growth of your social media page it's important to take time and celebrate the wins of the week as well as acknowledge anything that you may want to adjust for future use. Being aware of how your audience is responding to your content allows you to continue creating quality content that encourages engagement and ultimately leads to clients!

Why (Self Evaluation)
In the "why" section, this is where you take time to reflect on why your content performed well or why it did not perform well. What is your personal reflection on the previous week? Self reflection raises your level of awareness. Self reflection challenges you to be curious about what is and isn't working. It is also important to take personal responsibility

if the social media content didn't perform well, especially if you didn't do YOUR part.

Biz Goals For The Week

Let's get clear on our goal for the week ahead. Establish the specifics of your marketing efforts. What are you marketing? What is your income goal with the marketing efforts? And how are you going to market? Once you've established your marketing goals for the week you can begin creating quality content that will lead to conversion! Example: I need to enroll 2 new customers this week in my new course. Selling two courses will result in X amount of income. The next step is to make sure that I am creating my content for the week and it supports the enrollment of 2 new customers in my course.

The 4 Hash Method

When establishing your Unique Sharing Proposition let's take note of what your audience wants to hear from you! Remember, this is not what you sell, but part of who you are and how you connect to your audience. Think about it. There is a reason your audience started following you! It's kinda like dating. At first, you aren't quite sure what to expect, but as you begin to spend more time with that person, you decide whether you want to continue dating our bounce out! Just like dating, we aren't going to be everyone's cup of tea, right? However, when we consistently share who we are and what we stand for, our core values, and the things that matter to us, others are going to be able to decide if the initial connection is something they want to continue to pursue. Perhaps there is an initial connection, but to keep the audience coming back, we need to continue to convey that message. The initial connection is the REASON someone chooses to follow you and possibly purchase from you. If we aren't serving our audience content based on why they initially felt connected to us, they will likely unfollow or simply disconnect. Cultivating a comeback audience is consistently sharing content that is unique to you. Remember, when it comes to what you market: people will not follow you so much for WHAT YOU DO but WHY YOU DO IT.

Update: When we first created the *Make Chic Happen 52 Week Social Media Game Plan,* we incorporated the #4hashmethod. This is a way to identify the four main reasons someone engages with your content. These aren't hashtags you necessarily "use" (although you can). They more so reflect who you are and what you value most. Chances are there are certain types of content that you create which resonate well with your audience because they mean so much to you!

For example, when I prepare to post, I ask myself if it connects to one of these major themes:

However, we've decided to make a small adjustment to the #4hashmethod. It's important to note that there are a TON of people using (and marketing!) on social media, so to establish yourself as an influencer or a business owner in the space, we encourage clear credibility by leading with ONE MAIN #4hash. **Meaning, one of your MAIN #4hash should occur deliberately most often while the other major themes are consistent but less frequent.**

For example, if I want to be known as the go-to girl for all things #curvygirlfashion, I will choose to make that my MAIN theme that will be woven into my marketing the most often. I can use it to complement my other 4 themes, but it tends to show up in almost every post I do.

I call this the #4hashmethod. These are my BIG message musts. So when I prepare my content, I think of these 4 major hashtags that I would use to describe myself and my brand. When I post, I ask myself if the message connects to one of those 4 hashtags.

Let's try it! What are your 4 major hashtags? What is the big message you embed into your branding? What topics do you cover consistently? What does your audience seem to be most interested in? Define your #4hash here:

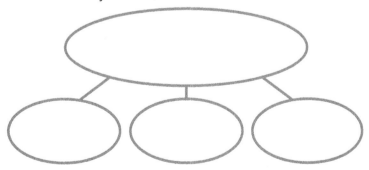

Pro Tip: As a social media branding rockstar, I highly suggest focusing on 3-4 major personal #4hash, with one of those being the primary focus! If we talk about too many topics, it becomes harder to cultivate true connection because our message becomes too broad.

EXAMPLE REFLECT & REFINE

Aug. 2, 2020
WEEK ENDING

f

POST REACH 5,882

CURRENT # OF FOLLOWERS 4,775

MOST ENGAGING POST

birthday post

SHARED / (ORIGINAL) (CIRCLE ONE)

(Instagram)

ACCOUNTS REACHED 25,215

NEW FOLLOWERS 70

CURRENT FOLLOWERS 17,945

HIGHEST POST REACH:

#makechichappen post

MOST SAVED CONTENT 62

MOST SHARED CONTENT 102 growth post

OF COLLABORATIONS 1

MOST STORY VIEWS 547

BUSINESS RESULTS

OF INVITES SENT? 100

OF CUSTOMERS ENROLLED? 5

INCOME I EARNED? $170

👍 WIN > 🌪 PLOT TWIST

- saved content (growth post) was 62
- collab with Fairmont helped us with new eyes

🤍 WHY (SELF EVALUATION)

- story views down b/c of update
- we can also be more diligent about tags and location

🎯 BIZ GOALS FOR THE WEEK

- we will add 10 new community members this week!

4 HASH METHOD

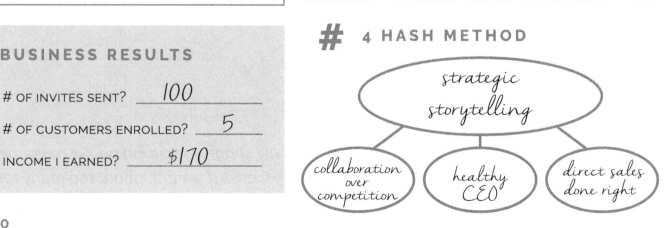

strategic storytelling

collaboration over competition

healthy CEO

direct sales done right

My Income Producing Activity (IPA) Tracker

We are so excited to introduce you to the next section of the planner. The "My Income Producing Activity Tracker" (IPA) section is essential to driving the results of your social media and income growth. We have learned over the years that anyone can make themselves "busy" doing work, but not everyone is busy doing the RIGHT work. The IPA tracker outlines the activities that you should be completing on a regular basis in order to get the results that you want. I know that tracking isn't necessarily the most glamorous and intsaworthy part of the job, but it is the ONLY way you will see success. If you don't know your trends, you won't know the truth embedded in your daily action. It's one thing to create content, but your content has to back up and support the private conversations you have with people. You NEED both conversations and social media content for success.

Let's break down the IPA tracker. The tasks listed are divided into three sections: community, conversion, and customer service. When these tasks are done consistently over time without the loss of enthusiasm, results compound.

Community

The first section is community. Community is where you are connecting and conversing with your ideal target audience.

Adding followers is defined as adding friends on Facebook or followers on Instagram that would fit your common interests, core values, and personality you previously defined in the **Signature Style** section. Adding followers can look like this: I go to my Facebook page where I search my kids' school district for a parents of X district closed Facebook group. I interact with parents in the group about common interests and send them a friend request. On Instagram, I might search #marsyouthbasketball and interact with other parents of players in our district. When I interact that might look like watching their stories and sending a direct message related to what they shared, commenting on a relevant post, and following the account. Growing my community is essential to building a healthy pipeline of future customers.

Intentional connection with followers is the next section. This is the part of the process where the person I engaged with in the first task responds back and we are in conversation. This is unrelated to my business. We are in the initial stages of developing a relationship. Think of this like going on a date. You are figuring out if this person is actually someone you want to continue connecting with. You are determining if you have the same core values and interests. You are not concerned about rushing to the invite process.

41

Creating your social media post(s) is the next task. This is creating social media content that is related to your #4hash method and connected to what your marketing goal for the week is.

We get asked all the time about how many pieces of content we should be sharing every day. Here is our rule of thumb. Ask yourself, "What does consistency look like for me?" Ask yourself, "How many times a day do I want to commit to showing up?" Then, you commit to that. For example, if you know that posting one time a day is what you can commit to, then DO IT, but do it consistently because IT MATTERS!!!

7-10 stories is the task of uploading stories to your Facebook and/or Instagram daily. Your stories are a peek behind the curtain of who you are. Your stories should be your daily call to action in your business, plus content that connects people to who you are and what you like and stand for. This is a great way to just share daily life, ask your audience for their feedback, and have fun conversation.

Highlight my customers, team members or other social media accounts. In this task you are focused on sharing social proof that what you provide works. Share testimonials, tag your current customers and product users, share relevant content that relates to your personality and style. Personally, I (Melanie) do this in my stories. Social proof is one of the best ways to build the know, like, and trust factor. This section allows you to move from "look at what I'm doing" to "YOU CAN DO IT TOO!"

Conversion

The second section of the IPA tracker is conversion. In this section, we are going to be focused on transitioning those initial conversations into invitations to the products and/or services that we have to offer.

DM (direct message) people who viewed, liked, commented on my stories and posts plus new followers. This task is where you are paying attention to who is engaging in your content and reaching out to start conversation. This is specific to what you sell or the services you offer.

For example, Sally voted on my poll about the free social media resource I created. I am going to message Sally and say, "Hey Sally, I saw you voted on my poll about the free social media resource. What is your email? I will send that right over to you!!!"

Direct invite to service, experience or product. This task means that you are going to be inviting people through private message to join you. Here is an example, "Hi Jenn, thanks so much for the love on my post about my online community. I currently have a spot in the community available if you would like the details. Let me know and I can get that right over to you."

Pro Tip: A good rule of thumb to follow is the 10% rule. Out of all the people you invite, 10% will say yes. Knowing the 10% rule allows you to back into the number of direct invites you need to send to get to your goal. For example, if I want to sign up 10 new community members this week, I need to send out 100 invites. I can split those invites up in any way that I would like.

Follow ups. This task is simple and straightforward. You are following up with all the people you have invited to your product, service, or experience. We recommend waiting 24 hours before sending the first follow up. Then, we follow up until registration closes, the product is sold out, or the person doesn't want to be on our list anymore.

Pro Tip: Most of our actual sales and conversions come in the follow up process. Don't ever discredit the power of consistent follow ups.

Ask for referrals. In this task you are going to your current customers and letting them know that you have another opportunity open for them to share with their friends and family. Asking for a referral can be done through a post in your VIP group, an email, a direct message, or text.

Customer Service
The last section of the tracker is customer service. In this section you are nurturing and supporting your current clients so that they become raving fans and refer you out for future business.

Engage with current clients. In this section you are setting aside time each day to engage with your current clients inside of your VIP group, private pages, or community platforms.

Answer emails and messages. This task is just simply reminding you to check your inbox and messages on social platforms for customer questions. Timely and individualized customer service does create trust and either allows people to move into raving fans for future referrals or, if you are in direct sales, sets the customer up to become a distributor.

Lastly, we have *business and personal development.* We added this to the tracker because if we don't understand the business we run and continually educate ourselves in the products and services our company offers then we won't be confident in sharing them online.

Educating ourselves about the business we own and how to do our jobs to the fullest potential has been essential to our exponential growth.

Personal development has also been a key area that we know has massively contributed to our business growth. As an entrepreneur we know that without constant mindset and leadership development we would not be able to scale the way that we have.

We encourage you to listen to audio books, podcasts, and read personal development books that empower you and teach you the skills needed to become the business owner you want to grow into.

See the free resources at ***https://chicinfluencer.com/free-resource***s for a list of our favorite personal development books, audios and podcasts

EXAMPLE MY INCOME PRODUCING ACTIVITY TRACKER

Aug. 2, 2020
WEEK OF

			Mon	Tues	Weds	Thur	Fri	Sat	Sun
INCOME PRODUCING ACTIVITIES	COMMUNITY	Add Followers	12	20	10	2	15	5	0
		Intentional Connect with Followers *not an invite	5	8	3	5	7	2	0
		Social Media Post (4 Hash Method)	1	1	1	1	1	1	1
		7-10 Stories	✓	✓	✓	✓	✓	✓	✓
		Highlight People: Testimonials/ Shout Outs	✓		✓		✓		
	CONVERSION	DM people who viewed, liked, commented, or followed	✓	✓	✓	✓	✓	✓	✓
		Direct invite to service, experience, or product	20	10	12	17	8	21	0
		Follow Ups	4	3	6	2	1	28	0
	CUSTOMER SERVICE	Ask for Referrals	1	1	3	0	4	1	0
		Engage with Current Clients	✓	✓	✓	✓	✓	✓	
		Answer Emails & Messages	✓	✓	✓	✓	✓	✓	
		Business Development	✓	✓	✓	✓	✓	✓	✓
		Personal Development	✓	✓	✓	✓		✓	

Weekly Marketing Plan

Let's get to work! On the next pages is your weekly calendar. You are going to organize your content ideas into day and platform (Facebook and Instagram). Here, you will put your content ideas and plug them into the stories or post sections. Make sure to write in how you will use this content in as many ways as possible. For example, if you create a post about an upcoming trunk sale, it might be a good idea to create an Instagram story set to compliment this marketing idea! Don't worry about making the spread perfect! We've left lots of room for you to create. We've included a few considerations for content as well!

Considerations for Content

Big Marketing Ideas to Carry into Content

You have a bottom line, so keep that at the front of your mind when preparing the weekly content! What is the message you are trying to convey to your audience? What services or products do you want to sell this week? Knowing that goal, what is the big idea that you want to drive home? Think about what you are trying to "do" with the content. For example, are you trying to sell a new line of mascara that has launched? Are you getting people into an event that you are hosting at your boutique? It's important to convey ONE big marketing idea to your audience at a time to avoid confusion.

Content Ideas

Once you've identified your goals and analyzed the weekly trends, it's time to get messy with new ideas, collaboration opportunities, potential roadblocks, and the FUN part of creating content for social media. We've created plenty of space within the weekly marketing calendar for you to write out your thoughts and get all of those reflections and creative ideas out onto paper! This is not the space to worry about "staying inside the lines." It's time to get messy with new ideas and get curious about improving past content! Think ahead about how you can lean into current events, trends, and the season! But don't forget, you are marketing with BOTTOM LINE intention. What is the big marketing idea that you are carrying into content? As long as you know what the marketing goal is for the week, we can keep that as a major focus for the week!

While brainstorming your content for the week, think about the purpose of the content you are creating. Ask yourself:

What is my marketing goal for the week?

Are there any current events or trends that I need to take into consideration?

What do I want to post about?

What elements of the #4hash can I consistently repeat to create a comeback audience?

What universal themes does my audience tend to interact with most?

We encourage you to write in pencil without permanency. Sometimes the plan is going to change, and that's ok! To help you brainstorm what the perfect piece of content will look like we've included a Content Checklist:
- Why are you creating this piece of content?
- Bold Tagline
- Personal Connection/Story
- Call to Think or Call to Act
- Image (eye-catching and matches the story)

Clarifying the purpose of your content
Whether you are directly marketing your products and services or adding value through storytelling, we recommend asking yourself the following questions before you post:

- What is the purpose of this content?
- How will this content benefit my audience?
    - Is it helpful?
    - Is it hopeful?
    - Is it healing?
- Is it aligned to my brand and my messaging?
- Can I align my content to my marketing goals?
- What do I want my audience to do with this particular piece of content?
- How am I measuring success with this particular piece of content?
    - Number of likes?
    - Action taken?
    - Comments left?
    - Conversations started?
    - Inventory moved?

Keeping Your Content "Reel"
Both Melanie and I (Katy) know how important social media is for marketing, but it's also a really fun way to share your ideas! It's important to use the updated features that a platform provides for you. For example, on Instagram, build into your marketing calendar the opportunity to create an IGTV, stories, reels, or incorporate other options (if applicable) such as creating a shop and sharing guides. Using available features is a great way to improve your visibility and share content in a new way! It's also important to note that people ENJOY content in different ways. While some of your audience may enjoy read-

ing your posts, others may engage more on LIVE content or a quick reel. If you want to **#makechichappen**, you can't be afraid to use new features! Embrace them, even if at first it feels like a flop!

Pro Tip: We always try to share one piece of content in three ways. That way we can refurbish quality content. You can write the taglines in the daily sections, or you can just write the idea for what you would like to post about. Ask yourself if this content would also make a great live video, IGTV, blog post, or brand email.

Implementing the Marketing Calendar

We use this calendar as our guide for what we will be sharing through the week. We do want to note that this is not a fixed plan. There will be times when you have a better idea that you want to swap out for another piece of content. Make sure you don't stay rigid in the approach but you allow yourself the flexibility to tweak the plan as your week progresses.

Let me (Melanie) explain why we feel so passionate about this weekly content plan. When you have a plan you are not working on the defense; you are working on the offense of your business. You are able to create content that is driving towards your business and social goals. You are even able to plan ahead with taking the photos for the post you want to make ahead of time. The weekly content planner has been a game changer for Chic Influencer, and we are so excited for you to dive in and get started.

You can see in the provided examples on the next few pages that I knew my outcome: to enroll X amount of people in my mentorship. I knew I had to serve first before I asked for a decision, and adding value is the best way to do that. You are not oversharing, you are not overdelivering, you are creating a trusting community where people will refer you to others because they know you are the real deal!

One last note: this is a work in progress. Blank spaces may happen from week to week. We encourage you to each week sit down and review your analytics and your content so that you are serving your audience exactly what they want to receive from you.

#MAKING *Chic* HAPPEN

CUSTOMER LOVE

Best planner I ever invested in, thank you for making this so specific! - Claudine

The #4hashmethod has really helped me focus my content. Oh and the #makechichappenplanner is a game changer!!! - Dawn Conder

Couldn't love mine any more! It's helping so much! - Lauren

My following has increased by 125% on both my Facebook Page and on Instagram. I know this is because I implemented this planner in January!! I have never been more consistent in my business, as well as, driven! I pursuing my dreams with purpose because of the structure and outline of this planner!
I love tracking my week ahead and knowing exactly what I'm going to post each day. I love that I pay attention to my insights now and I can see what's working and what isn't! I love looking ahead each month at what I need to start promoting and when. This planner has been life changing. I'm so incredibly grateful for this! My business has never been better and I only see it continuing to grow from here!
- Erica Yeager

EXAMPLE WEEKLY SOCIAL MEDIA PLAN

THINGS TO CONSIDER

- Captions/Taglines
- Content I Like
- Hashtags
- Objections
- Collaborations
- Pain Points
- Well Received Content to Refurbish
- CTA's
- CTT's
- Quotables
- Community Driven Content
- Upcoming Events

CONTENT CREATION CHECKLIST

- ☐ Why are you creating this piece of content?
- ☐ Bold Tagline
- ☐ Personal connection/story
- ☐ Call to Think or Call to Act
- ☐ Image (eye-catching and matches the story)

	MONDAY	TUESDAY	WEDNESDAY
f FACEBOOK	CTA (call to act) for chic your gram shared blog post related to social media	testimonial "chic your gram"	funny meme (same as IG) fear of investing in biz (live)
INSTAGRAM	CTA for chic your gram	testimonial "chic your gram" CTA > bio	funny meme "algorithm" w/ tagline about not being seen
IG STORIES	shared blog post announcing enrollment is open	testimonial CTA > swipe up	share post "investing in your biz" CTA

THURSDAY	FRIDAY	SATURDAY	SUNDAY
f	**f**	**f**	**f**
podcast	share live to FB	"biggest mistake we see marketers make"	# of spots left CTA
fear of investing in biz	evening post: purposeful rest, unplug		
great tagline			create good images shared blog post
shared blog post			
ⓘ	ⓘ	ⓘ	ⓘ
podcast	share live to IGTV	"biggest mistake we see marketers make"	swipe 10 must follow accounts
fear of investing in biz			
⊕	⊕	⊕	⊕
podcast	live: how to cultivate community - turn into IGTV and FB	pull from post 4 IG stories	10 must follow accounts
shared blog post		_____	
share post	purposeful rest tips	how many spots left? snag yours!	

EXAMPLE 1

Monday: We will create a live video on IGTV where we talk about why we're passionate about our business and who we love to serve the most. Talk about your story, connect to your audience, and keep it under five minutes. Turn that one video into an IGTV with a CTA (call to action). One thing that we do is always ask ourselves what do we want people to do with this content we've created?

Then we refurbish the content:
Take that video and put it on your FB page with a CTA.
Take that video and share it through an email to your list of potential customers with a story about you!
Take the bullet points and make an IG story directing them to the IGTV video.

See?! We just created one video and found three different ways to share one idea. HOLY TIME SAVER, right?!

Pro Tip: We always ask ourselves how can we stretch this ONE piece of content? How can we continue to drive home the BIG idea on multiple platforms while making the most of our time?

Remember, it typically takes us about 10-14 days to drive home a particular concept before our audience starts to "lean in", ask questions, and pursue our services. We STRONGLY encourage you to NOT get discouraged if you don't see immediate results. If you are committed and willing to make adjustments as you go, this strategy is highly effective. We don't get mad when something isn't working in our favor, we get curious about how we can do better.

When it comes to creating content, make sure your content is not always HARD CALLS TO SELL. People tune out product pushers. Add value in your content; serve, don't sell!

We at Chic follow this style: add value, add value, add value, add value, ask for a decision!

EXAMPLE 2: My goal is to sign up three new clients to my private mentorship focused on creating loyal followers. Refer back to Reflect and Refine and ask yourself what is your desired outcome this week?
- Make X amount of sales?
- Get X amount of new followers?
- Get X amount of engagement?

Chic'ing It, Not Winging It

Let's be honest for a moment. There will be weeks that you won't have a lot of time to do your planning. There will be weeks when the ideas are not flowing as creatively as you would like. There will be times when you are in a crunch for time. That is ok! What is NOT OK is for you to push your social media planner aside and NOT have a game plan. Every time I fail to plan, I am planning to fail!!

So what does chic'ing it look like?

On weeks where you have to sorta kinda wing it, pull out your planner and do some basic work. Here are a few of our tips to avoid scrambling for content:
   • Write down your focus for the week and what goals you know you need to drive towards.
   • Then, jot down your taglines and some post ideas. Set some realistic social media goals for the week and definitely reflect on what is and isn't working for your social media at this time.
   • Be intentional, even if you are intentionally winging it!

Try to steer clear of JUST GOING THROUGH THE MOTIONS and documenting your day or checking off the social media boxes. Ask yourself, "Am I posting to just throw up a post? What is the purpose of the content that I am about to share?"

This simple gut check will make sure you stay focused on your north star (AKA your goals) and keep you from becoming white noise. Both Katy and I go by the rule of thumb that it is better to post nothing at all than to throw something up just to say you posted. That will never serve your ultimate goal.

Time Blocking

Alright friends, we are moving into my (Melanie's) wheelhouse. I added this section to the planner because you can create the most well thought out content plan, but if you don't create intentional space in your week to get the work done, then you are going to be spinning your wheels.

When I decided to get serious about growing my business, the first thing I did was create a weekly schedule for myself that was broken down by the hour.

If I was going to reach my business goals I was going to have to make time for the activities. Every Sunday I have a planning session with myself to review content, to review my goals, and to create a plan for the upcoming week. I start by putting on the time blocking tracker all of the commitments, appointments, and meetings that are set in stone. My kids' sports practices, our weekly team meetings, standing business meetings, and more. Next, I write in my personal business blocks of time. When my boys were little I would block off the afternoon nap times as "work time" and the evenings after they went to bed as my dedicated "work time". I would go through my entire week and block off the times dedicated to growing this business. Then, I would write in my personal time. For example, I wake up at 5:00 am because I like having a quiet space to read, to do my morning gratitude, and to exercise. I put in space for my shower, breakfast, and then the start to the work day. I also block off time for date nights, movie nights, and unplugged time from my work. Let's face it, when you run an online business it can feel like you are always attached to it. I create intentional space where I am unplugged to purposefully recharge.

After I finish my calendar, I will share my plans with my husband since we both have to divide and conquer when it comes to running a business and managing our family. We talk about challenges that we will face during the week, what each of us has to do to make all ends meet, and then we do our best to make sure that we communicate so that everything is taken care of.

We have attached sample time blocking calendars on the next few pages for you to see how a week looks for both myself and Katy. We wanted to give you two different examples of how the time blocking tracker is used. I (Melanie) am sharing as someone who is building their business full time. The second example is when Katy was working full-time as a teacher and building her business in the pockets of free time. Katy would use her commute to and from work to listen to podcasts, catch up on team calls, or trainings. You will see that she has blocked off her work hours where she is completely unavailable. We wanted to show you how the time blocker works no matter what your current situation is.

Space in your time blocker that is blank is what we refer to as "white space". There isn't anything in particular planned during those times on purpose because we want to create wiggle room and flexibility because we know life does happen! We give ourselves grace and do our best not to over commit and pack our schedules too full if we can help it. These time blocking trackers have been our saving grace in keeping our priorities in check and our focus on what matters most.

We also have a sheet that you can download for yourself and use for your own weekly tracking. You can find that resource at *https://chicinfluencer.com/free-resources.*

When you connect your goals to your time blocking tracker, everything begins to work together which gives you more control and peace about the process.

KATY'S TIME BLOCKING TRACKER EXAMPLE

Aug. 2, 2020
WEEK OF

NOTES

_____
_____
_____
_____
_____
_____
_____
_____
_____
_____
_____
_____
_____
_____
_____

MONTHLY GOALS

$660 in commissions

WEEKLY GOALS

$165 in commissions

	MONDAY	TUESDAY	WEDNESDAY
5 am	workout, Back	Pocket Prayer time, biz dev	
6 am	check in with	group, schedule content	
7 am	personal biz time (list activites here)	personal biz time (list activites here)	personal biz time (list activites here)
8 am			
9 am	Katy at work	Katy at work	Katy at work
10 am			
11 pm			
12 pm	customer service/ emails/ team	customer service/ emails/ team	customer service/ emails/ team
1 pm			
2 pm	Katy at work	Katy at work	Katy at work
3 pm			
4 pm	invites / biz/personal development	invites / biz/personal development	invites / biz/personal development
5 pm			
6 pm	family time	family time	family time
7 pm			
8 pm	content creation	content creation	biz opportunity
9 pm	team call	check in w/ team	follow up
10 pm	bed time		

	THURSDAY	FRIDAY	SATURDAY	SUNDAY
5 am				
6 am				
7 am	personal biz time (list activites here)	personal biz time (list activites here)	fit club	prep for week and prep content for week
8 am				
9 am	Katy at work	Katy at work		
10 am				
11 pm				
12 pm	customer service/ emails/ team	customer service/ emails/ team	family time	
1 pm				
2 pm	Katy at work	Katy at work		
3 pm				family time
4 pm	invites / biz/personal development	invites / biz/personal development	check ins	
5 pm				
6 pm	date night		content creation	
7 pm		family time		
8 pm	check in w/ team			
9 pm				check in w/ client; schedule week ahead
10 pm				

MEL'S TIME BLOCKING TRACKER EXAMPLE

Aug. 2, 2020
_____
WEEK OF

NOTES

_____
_____
_____
_____
_____
_____
_____
_____
_____
_____
_____
_____

MONTHLY GOALS

$1200 in commissions

WEEKLY GOALS

$300 in commissions

	MONDAY	TUESDAY	WEDNESDAY
5 am	personal dev/ workout/ prep for day	personal dev/ workout/ prep for day	personal dev/ workout/ prep for day
6 am			
7 am			
8 am		team call	
9 am	personal biz time (list activites here)	personal biz time (list activites here)	
10 am			doctor's appt
11 am			
12 pm	leadership call	clean up the house!	personal biz time (list activites here)
1 pm			
2 pm	customer service/ emails/ team	customer service/ emails/ team	family time
3 pm			
4 pm			
5 pm	family time	family time/ grocery store	customer service/ emails/ team
6 pm			
7 pm			
8 pm	team call	finish any loose ends and set tasks for next day	finish any loose ends and set tasks for next day
9 pm			
10 pm	bedtime		

	THURSDAY	FRIDAY	SATURDAY	SUNDAY
5 am	personal time/ workout/ reading	personal dev/ workout/prep for day	personal dev/ workout/prep for day	
6 am				
7 am				
8 am	personal biz time (list activites here)	personal biz time (list activites here)	personal biz time (list activites here)	personal biz time (list activites here)
9 am				
10 am	leader call	customer service/emails/ team		weekly planning / reflection
11 am				
12 pm	mentorship call		customer service/emails/ team	
1 pm	blog post			
2 pm				
3 pm	live w/ evereve			family time
4 pm	email msgs			
5 pm	customer service		family time	
6 pm				
7 pm		family movie night		
8 pm				finish any loose ends and set tasks for next day
9 pm				
10 pm				

YOUR TIME BLOCKING TRACKER EXAMPLE

WEEK OF

NOTES

_____
_____
_____
_____
_____
_____
_____
_____
_____
_____
_____
_____
_____
_____

MONTHLY GOALS

WEEKLY GOALS

	MONDAY	TUESDAY	WEDNESDAY
5 am			
6 am			
7 am			
8 am			
9 am			
10 am			
11 pm			
12 pm			
1 pm			
2 pm			
3 pm			
4 pm			
5 pm			
6 pm			
7 pm			
8 pm			
9 pm			
10 pm			

	THURSDAY	FRIDAY	SATURDAY	SUNDAY
5 am				
6 am				
7 am				
8 am				
9 am				
10 am				
11 pm				
12 pm				
1 pm				
2 pm				
3 pm				
4 pm				
5 pm				
6 pm				
7 pm				
8 pm				
9 pm				
10 pm				

3

#Chic IT UP

Take your marketing to the next level with these resources!

23 CONTENT STARTERS

On the path to **#makechichappen**, it's ok if you are lacking creativity. It doesn't always come naturally to us either! If you need to create a post, but your creativity is lacking, simply use these content ideas to get things flowing!

- Introductory Post
- How To Tutorial
- Promote A Product You Swear By
- Spotify Playlist For Current Mood
- Workout And Why
- Share Your Story
- Answer An Objection/Common Concern
- Provide A Tip
- Feature Service Or Product
- Giveaway
- Shout Out To Clients/ Team Members
- Inspiration Quote
- Workspace
- Current Reads
- Hobby
- Business Buddy Shout Out
- Testimonial
- Gratitude
- Behind The Scenes
- Shared Content (Note: make sure you give proper credit)
- Funny Meme
- Personal Testimonial
- Personal Story

FAVORITE MAKE CHIC HAPPEN PODCAST EPISODES FOR CREATING CONTENT

- Episode 72: The 5 Questions to Ask Yourself When Connecting with Your Audience
- Episode 70: Why Losing Followers is a GOOD Thing When You Want to Grow
- Episode 66: How Katy REALLY Created the Post that Got Over 100,000 Shares on Facebook

TOP 5 MUST-HAVE APPS TO ROCK INSTAGRAM

Melanie and I get by with a little help from our apps when it comes to ROCKING our Instagram. Below is a list of 5 of our favorite apps.

- LightRoom
- PLANN
- Instastories
- Unfold
- Word Swag

To learn more about how we use each of these apps head over to *https://chicinfluencer.com/free-resources* and select **#makechichappen!**

HASHTAG SETS

Start with the #4hashmethod. Write each of your personal hashtags in the boxes across the top. Then, below each personal tag, create your list of relevant and related hashtags. PRO-TIP: Use pencil. This is something you will refine often. Remember, hashtags are like a card catalog in a library, every hashtag catalogs your post in that specific category. The post becomes searchable and connects back to the content you've created. Remember, you want to use hashtags that are specific to your ideal audience and use hashtags that relate to the content you posted about. Don't forget that using hashtags in your content is only part of the work! ENGAGE with those who are using similar hashtags to more deeply connect!

HASHTAG SET >				
1				
2				
3				
4				
5				
6				
7				
8				
9				
10				
11				
12				
13				
14				
15				
16				
17				
18				
19				
20				
21				
22				
23				
24				
25				
26				
27				

NOW IT'S YOUR TURN TO...

#MAKE
Chic
HAPPEN

4

month:

_____

marketing focus:

_____

_____

_____

_____

_____

_____

_____

_____

_____

_____

MONDAY	TUESDAY	WEDNESDAY

MONTHLY GOALS:

THURSDAY	FRIDAY	SATURDAY	SUNDAY

REFLECT & REFINE

POST REACH ∧∨ _____

CURRENT # OF FOLLOWERS ∧∨ _____

MOST ENGAGING POST _____

_____

_____

SHARED / ORIGINAL (CIRCLE ONE)

👍 WIN > 🌪 PLOT TWIST

♡ WHY (SELF EVALUATION)

ACCOUNTS REACHED ∧∨ _____

NEW FOLLOWERS _____

CURRENT FOLLOWERS _____

HIGHEST POST REACH:

_____

MOST SAVED CONTENT _____

MOST SHARED CONTENT _____

OF COLLABORATIONS _____

MOST STORY VIEWS _____

🎯 BIZ GOALS FOR THE WEEK

BUSINESS RESULTS

OF INVITES SENT? _____

OF CUSTOMERS ENROLLED? _____

INCOME I EARNED? _____

4 HASH METHOD

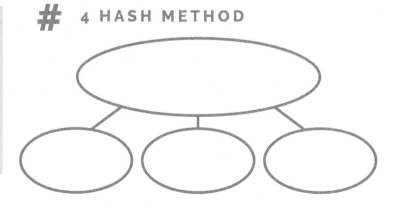

MY INCOME PRODUCING
ACTIVITY TRACKER

			Mon	Tues	Weds	Thur	Fri	Sat	Sun
INCOME PRODUCING ACTIVITIES	**COMMUNITY**	Add Followers							
		Intentional Connect with Followers *not an invite							
		Social Media Post (4 Hash Method)							
		7-10 Stories							
		Highlight People: Testimonials/ Shout Outs							
	CONVERSION	DM people who viewed, liked, commented, or followed							
		Direct invite to service, experience, or product							
		Follow Ups							
	CUSTOMER SERVICE	Ask for Referrals							
		Engage with Current Clients							
		Answer Emails & Messages							
		Business Development							
		Personal Development							

WEEKLY SOCIAL MEDIA PLAN

THINGS TO CONSIDER

- Captions/Taglines
- Content I Like
- Hashtags
- Objections
- Collaborations
- Pain Points
- Well Received Content to Refurbish
- CTA's
- CTT's
- Quotables
- Community Driven Content
- Upcoming Events

CONTENT CREATION CHECKLIST

- ☐ Why are you creating this piece of content?
- ☐ Bold Tagline
- ☐ Personal connection/story
- ☐ Call to Think or Call to Act
- ☐ Image (eye-catching and matches the story)

MONDAY	TUESDAY	WEDNESDAY
f FACEBOOK	**f**	**f**
⊙ INSTAGRAM	⊙	⊙
⊕ IG STORIES	⊕	⊕

THURSDAY	FRIDAY	SATURDAY	SUNDAY
f	f	f	f
o	o	o	o
(+)	(+)	(+)	(+)

REFLECT & REFINE

f

POST REACH ^v _____

CURRENT # OF FOLLOWERS ^v _____

MOST ENGAGING POST _____

_____

_____

SHARED / ORIGINAL (CIRCLE ONE)

👍 WIN > 🌪 PLOT TWIST

🤍 WHY (SELF EVALUATION)

🎯 BIZ GOALS FOR THE WEEK

📷 (Instagram)

ACCOUNTS REACHED ^v _____

NEW FOLLOWERS _____

CURRENT FOLLOWERS _____

HIGHEST POST REACH:

_____

MOST SAVED CONTENT _____

MOST SHARED CONTENT _____

OF COLLABORATIONS _____

MOST STORY VIEWS _____

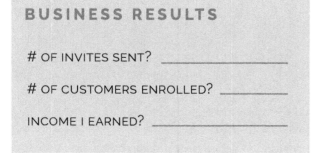

BUSINESS RESULTS

OF INVITES SENT? _____

OF CUSTOMERS ENROLLED? _____

INCOME I EARNED? _____

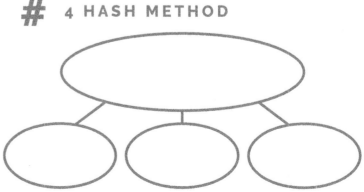

4 HASH METHOD

MY INCOME PRODUCING ACTIVITY TRACKER

WEEK OF

		Mon	Tues	Weds	Thur	Fri	Sat	Sun
INCOME PRODUCING ACTIVITIES	**COMMUNITY**	Add Followers						
		Intentional Connect with Followers *not an invite						
		Social Media Post (4 Hash Method)						
		7-10 Stories						
		Highlight People: Testimonials/ Shout Outs						
	CONVERSION	DM people who viewed, liked, commented, or followed						
		Direct invite to service, experience, or product						
		Follow Ups						
	CUSTOMER SERVICE	Ask for Referrals						
		Engage with Current Clients						
		Answer Emails & Messages						
		Business Development						
		Personal Development						

WEEKLY SOCIAL MEDIA PLAN

THINGS TO CONSIDER

- Captions/Taglines
- Content I Like
- Hashtags
- Objections
- Collaborations
- Pain Points
- Well Received
  Content to Refurbish
- CTA's
- CTT's
- Quotables
- Community Driven
  Content
- Upcoming Events

CONTENT CREATION CHECKLIST

- [ ] Why are you creating this piece of content?
- [ ] Bold Tagline
- [ ] Personal connection/story
- [ ] Call to Think or Call to Act
- [ ] Image (eye-catching and matches the story)

MONDAY	TUESDAY	WEDNESDAY
f FACEBOOK	**f**	**f**
⬡ INSTAGRAM	⬡	⬡
⊕ IG STORIES	⊕	⊕

MY GOAL THIS WEEK:

THURSDAY	FRIDAY	SATURDAY	SUNDAY
f	f	f	f
⊙	⊙	⊙	⊙
⊕	⊕	⊕	⊕

REFLECT & REFINE

f _____

POST REACH ⋀⋁ _____

CURRENT # OF FOLLOWERS ⋀⋁ _____

MOST ENGAGING POST _____

_____

_____

SHARED / ORIGINAL (CIRCLE ONE)

👍 WIN > 🌪 PLOT TWIST

🤍 WHY (SELF EVALUATION)

🎯 BIZ GOALS FOR THE WEEK

📷

ACCOUNTS REACHED ⋀⋁ _____

NEW FOLLOWERS _____

CURRENT FOLLOWERS _____

HIGHEST POST REACH:

_____

MOST SAVED CONTENT _____

MOST SHARED CONTENT _____

OF COLLABORATIONS _____

MOST STORY VIEWS _____

BUSINESS RESULTS

OF INVITES SENT? _____

OF CUSTOMERS ENROLLED? _____

INCOME I EARNED? _____

---

4 HASH METHOD

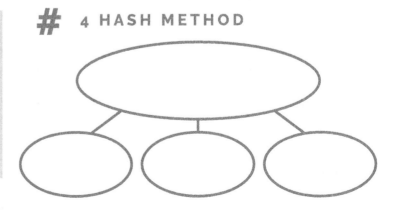

MY INCOME PRODUCING
ACTIVITY TRACKER

			Mon	Tues	Weds	Thur	Fri	Sat	Sun
INCOME PRODUCING ACTIVITIES	**COMMUNITY**	Add Followers							
		Intentional Connect with Followers *not an invite							
		Social Media Post (4 Hash Method)							
		7-10 Stories							
		Highlight People: Testimonials/ Shout Outs							
	CONVERSION	DM people who viewed, liked, commented, or followed							
		Direct invite to service, experience, or product							
		Follow Ups							
	CUSTOMER SERVICE	Ask for Referrals							
		Engage with Current Clients							
		Answer Emails & Messages							
		Business Development							
		Personal Development							

WEEKLY SOCIAL MEDIA PLAN

THINGS TO CONSIDER

- Captions/Taglines
- Content I Like
- Hashtags
- Objections
- Collaborations
- Pain Points
- Well Received Content to Refurbish
- CTA's
- CTT's
- Quotables
- Community Driven Content
- Upcoming Events

CONTENT CREATION CHECKLIST

- ☐ Why are you creating this piece of content?
- ☐ Bold Tagline
- ☐ Personal connection/story
- ☐ Call to Think or Call to Act
- ☐ Image (eye-catching and matches the story)

MONDAY	TUESDAY	WEDNESDAY
f FACEBOOK	**f**	**f**
ⓞ INSTAGRAM	ⓞ	ⓞ
⊕ IG STORIES	⊕	⊕

MY GOAL THIS WEEK:

THURSDAY	FRIDAY	SATURDAY	SUNDAY
f	f	f	f
ⓞ	ⓞ	ⓞ	ⓞ
⊕	⊕	⊕	⊕

REFLECT & REFINE

f

POST REACH ^∨ _____

CURRENT # OF FOLLOWERS ^∨ _____

MOST ENGAGING POST _____

_____

_____

SHARED / ORIGINAL (CIRCLE ONE)

(Instagram)

ACCOUNTS REACHED ^∨ _____

NEW FOLLOWERS _____

CURRENT FOLLOWERS _____

HIGHEST POST REACH:

_____

MOST SAVED CONTENT _____

MOST SHARED CONTENT _____

OF COLLABORATIONS _____

MOST STORY VIEWS _____

BUSINESS RESULTS

OF INVITES SENT? _____

OF CUSTOMERS ENROLLED? _____

INCOME I EARNED? _____

WEEK ENDING

👍 WIN > 🌪 PLOT TWIST

♡ WHY (SELF EVALUATION)

🎯 BIZ GOALS FOR THE WEEK

4 HASH METHOD

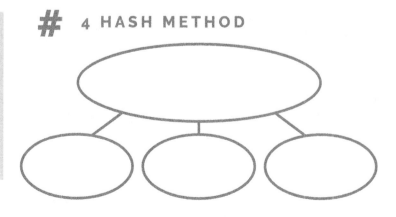

MY INCOME PRODUCING ACTIVITY TRACKER

WEEK OF

		Mon	Tues	Weds	Thur	Fri	Sat	Sun
INCOME PRODUCING ACTIVITIES	**COMMUNITY**	Add Followers						
		Intentional Connect with Followers *not an invite						
		Social Media Post (4 Hash Method)						
		7-10 Stories						
		Highlight People: Testimonials/ Shout Outs						
	CONVERSION	DM people who viewed, liked, commented, or followed						
		Direct invite to service, experience, or product						
		Follow Ups						
	CUSTOMER SERVICE	Ask for Referrals						
		Engage with Current Clients						
		Answer Emails & Messages						
		Business Development						
		Personal Development						

WEEKLY SOCIAL MEDIA PLAN

THINGS TO CONSIDER

- Captions/Taglines
- Content I Like
- Hashtags
- Objections
- Collaborations
- Pain Points
- Well Received Content to Refurbish
- CTA's
- CTT's
- Quotables
- Community Driven Content
- Upcoming Events

CONTENT CREATION CHECKLIST

- ☐ Why are you creating this piece of content?
- ☐ Bold Tagline
- ☐ Personal connection/story
- ☐ Call to Think or Call to Act
- ☐ Image (eye-catching and matches the story)

MONDAY	TUESDAY	WEDNESDAY
f FACEBOOK	**f**	**f**
⬡ INSTAGRAM	⬡	⬡
⊕ IG STORIES	⊕	⊕

THURSDAY	FRIDAY	SATURDAY	SUNDAY
f	f	f	f
⊙	⊙	⊙	⊙
⊕	⊕	⊕	⊕

REFLECT & REFINE

f

POST REACH ∧∨ _____

CURRENT # OF FOLLOWERS ∧∨ _____

MOST ENGAGING POST _____

_____

_____

SHARED / ORIGINAL (CIRCLE ONE)

WEEK ENDING

👍 WIN > 🌪 PLOT TWIST

♡ WHY (SELF EVALUATION)

🎯 BIZ GOALS FOR THE WEEK

⚪ (Instagram)

ACCOUNTS REACHED ∧∨ _____

NEW FOLLOWERS _____

CURRENT FOLLOWERS _____

HIGHEST POST REACH:

_____

MOST SAVED CONTENT _____

MOST SHARED CONTENT _____

OF COLLABORATIONS _____

MOST STORY VIEWS _____

BUSINESS RESULTS

OF INVITES SENT? _____

OF CUSTOMERS ENROLLED? _____

INCOME I EARNED? _____

4 HASH METHOD

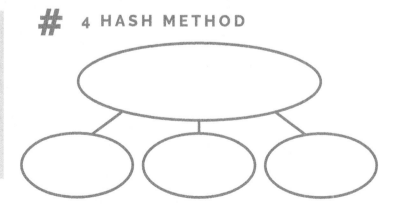

MY INCOME PRODUCING
ACTIVITY TRACKER

		Mon	Tues	Weds	Thur	Fri	Sat	Sun
INCOME PRODUCING ACTIVITIES	**COMMUNITY**	Add Followers						
		Intentional Connect with Followers *not an invite						
		Social Media Post (4 Hash Method)						
		7-10 Stories						
		Highlight People: Testimonials/ Shout Outs						
	CONVERSION	DM people who viewed, liked, commented, or followed						
		Direct invite to service, experience, or product						
		Follow Ups						
	CUSTOMER SERVICE	Ask for Referrals						
		Engage with Current Clients						
		Answer Emails & Messages						
		Business Development						
		Personal Development						

WEEKLY SOCIAL MEDIA PLAN

THINGS TO CONSIDER

- Captions/Taglines
- Content I Like
- Hashtags
- Objections
- Collaborations
- Pain Points
- Well Received Content to Refurbish
- CTA's
- CTT's
- Quotables
- Community Driven Content
- Upcoming Events

CONTENT CREATION CHECKLIST

- ☐ Why are you creating this piece of content?
- ☐ Bold Tagline
- ☐ Personal connection/story
- ☐ Call to Think or Call to Act
- ☐ Image (eye-catching and matches the story)

MONDAY	TUESDAY	WEDNESDAY
f FACEBOOK	**f**	**f**
ⓘ INSTAGRAM	ⓘ	ⓘ
⊕ IG STORIES	⊕	⊕

MY GOAL THIS WEEK:

THURSDAY	FRIDAY	SATURDAY	SUNDAY
f	f	f	f
⊙	⊙	⊙	⊙
⊕	⊕	⊕	⊕

month:

_____

*marketing
focus:*

_____

_____

_____

_____

_____

_____

_____

_____

_____

_____

_____

MONDAY	TUESDAY	WEDNESDAY

MONTHLY GOALS:

THURSDAY	FRIDAY	SATURDAY	SUNDAY

REFLECT & REFINE

f

POST REACH ∧∨ _____

CURRENT # OF FOLLOWERS ∧∨ _____

MOST ENGAGING POST _____

_____

_____

SHARED / ORIGINAL (CIRCLE ONE)

(Instagram)

ACCOUNTS REACHED ∧∨ _____

NEW FOLLOWERS _____

CURRENT FOLLOWERS _____

HIGHEST POST REACH:

_____

MOST SAVED CONTENT _____

MOST SHARED CONTENT _____

OF COLLABORATIONS _____

MOST STORY VIEWS _____

BUSINESS RESULTS

OF INVITES SENT? _____

OF CUSTOMERS ENROLLED? _____

INCOME I EARNED? _____

_____

WEEK ENDING

👍 WIN > 🌪 PLOT TWIST

♡ WHY (SELF EVALUATION)

🎯 BIZ GOALS FOR THE WEEK

4 HASH METHOD

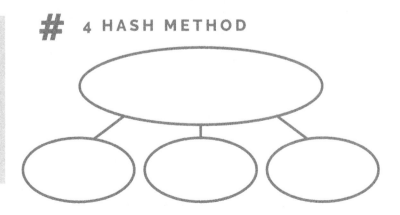

MY INCOME PRODUCING ACTIVITY TRACKER

		Mon	Tues	Weds	Thur	Fri	Sat	Sun
INCOME PRODUCING ACTIVITIES	**COMMUNITY**	Add Followers						
		Intentional Connect with Followers *not an invite						
		Social Media Post (4 Hash Method)						
		7-10 Stories						
		Highlight People: Testimonials/ Shout Outs						
	CONVERSION	DM people who viewed, liked, commented, or followed						
		Direct invite to service, experience, or product						
		Follow Ups						
	CUSTOMER SERVICE	Ask for Referrals						
		Engage with Current Clients						
		Answer Emails & Messages						
		Business Development						
		Personal Development						

WEEKLY SOCIAL MEDIA PLAN

THINGS TO CONSIDER

- Captions/Taglines
- Content I Like
- Hashtags
- Objections
- Collaborations
- Pain Points
- Well Received Content to Refurbish
- CTA's
- CTT's
- Quotables
- Community Driven Content
- Upcoming Events

CONTENT CREATION CHECKLIST

- ☐ Why are you creating this piece of content?
- ☐ Bold Tagline
- ☐ Personal connection/story
- ☐ Call to Think or Call to Act
- ☐ Image (eye-catching and matches the story)

MONDAY	TUESDAY	WEDNESDAY
f FACEBOOK	**f**	**f**
⃝ INSTAGRAM	⃝	⃝
⊕ IG STORIES	⊕	⊕

THURSDAY	FRIDAY	SATURDAY	SUNDAY
f	f	f	f
⊙	⊙	⊙	⊙
⊕	⊕	⊕	⊕

REFLECT & REFINE

f

POST REACH ∧∨ _____

CURRENT # OF FOLLOWERS ∧∨ _____

MOST ENGAGING POST _____

_____

_____

SHARED / ORIGINAL (CIRCLE ONE)

[Instagram icon]

ACCOUNTS REACHED ∧∨ _____

NEW FOLLOWERS _____

CURRENT FOLLOWERS _____

HIGHEST POST REACH:

_____

MOST SAVED CONTENT _____

MOST SHARED CONTENT _____

OF COLLABORATIONS _____

MOST STORY VIEWS _____

BUSINESS RESULTS

OF INVITES SENT? _____

OF CUSTOMERS ENROLLED? _____

INCOME I EARNED? _____

WEEK ENDING

👍 WIN > 🌪 PLOT TWIST

♡ WHY (SELF EVALUATION)

🎯 BIZ GOALS FOR THE WEEK

4 HASH METHOD

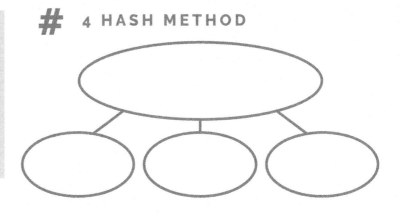

MY INCOME PRODUCING ACTIVITY TRACKER

WEEK OF _____

		Mon	Tues	Weds	Thur	Fri	Sat	Sun
INCOME PRODUCING ACTIVITIES	**COMMUNITY**	Add Followers						
		Intentional Connect with Followers *not an invite						
		Social Media Post (4 Hash Method)						
		7-10 Stories						
		Highlight People: Testimonials/ Shout Outs						
	CONVERSION	DM people who viewed, liked, commented, or followed						
		Direct invite to service, experience, or product						
		Follow Ups						
	CUSTOMER SERVICE	Ask for Referrals						
		Engage with Current Clients						
		Answer Emails & Messages						
		Business Development						
		Personal Development						

WEEKLY SOCIAL MEDIA PLAN

THINGS TO CONSIDER

- Captions/Taglines
- Content I Like
- Hashtags
- Objections
- Collaborations
- Pain Points
- Well Received Content to Refurbish
- CTA's
- CTT's
- Quotables
- Community Driven Content
- Upcoming Events

CONTENT CREATION CHECKLIST

- ☐ Why are you creating this piece of content?
- ☐ Bold Tagline
- ☐ Personal connection/story
- ☐ Call to Think or Call to Act
- ☐ Image (eye-catching and matches the story)

	MONDAY	TUESDAY	WEDNESDAY
f FACEBOOK		f	f
⊙ INSTAGRAM		⊙	⊙
⊕ IG STORIES		⊕	⊕

MY GOAL THIS WEEK:

THURSDAY	FRIDAY	SATURDAY	SUNDAY
f	f	f	f
⃝	⃝	⃝	⃝
⊕	⊕	⊕	⊕

REFLECT & REFINE

f

POST REACH ⌃⌄ _____

CURRENT # OF FOLLOWERS ⌃⌄ _____

MOST ENGAGING POST _____

_____

_____

SHARED / ORIGINAL (CIRCLE ONE)

⌾

ACCOUNTS REACHED ⌃⌄ _____

NEW FOLLOWERS _____

CURRENT FOLLOWERS _____

HIGHEST POST REACH:

_____

MOST SAVED CONTENT _____

MOST SHARED CONTENT _____

OF COLLABORATIONS _____

MOST STORY VIEWS _____

BUSINESS RESULTS

OF INVITES SENT? _____

OF CUSTOMERS ENROLLED? _____

INCOME I EARNED? _____

WEEK ENDING

👍 WIN > 🌪 PLOT TWIST

♡ WHY (SELF EVALUATION)

◎ BIZ GOALS FOR THE WEEK

4 HASH METHOD

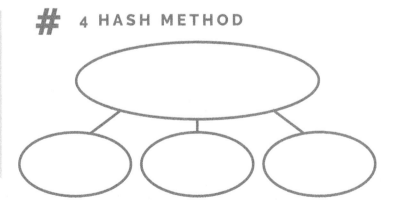

MY INCOME PRODUCING ACTIVITY TRACKER

			Mon	Tues	Weds	Thur	Fri	Sat	Sun
INCOME PRODUCING ACTIVITIES	**COMMUNITY**	Add Followers							
		Intentional Connect with Followers *not an invite							
		Social Media Post (4 Hash Method)							
		7-10 Stories							
		Highlight People: Testimonials/ Shout Outs							
	CONVERSION	DM people who viewed, liked, commented, or followed							
		Direct invite to service, experience, or product							
		Follow Ups							
	CUSTOMER SERVICE	Ask for Referrals							
		Engage with Current Clients							
		Answer Emails & Messages							
		Business Development							
		Personal Development							

WEEKLY SOCIAL MEDIA PLAN

THINGS TO CONSIDER

- Captions/Taglines
- Content I Like
- Hashtags
- Objections
- Collaborations
- Pain Points
- Well Received Content to Refurbish
- CTA's
- CTT's
- Quotables
- Community Driven Content
- Upcoming Events

CONTENT CREATION CHECKLIST

- ☐ Why are you creating this piece of content?
- ☐ Bold Tagline
- ☐ Personal connection/story
- ☐ Call to Think or Call to Act
- ☐ Image (eye-catching and matches the story)

MONDAY	TUESDAY	WEDNESDAY
f FACEBOOK	**f**	**f**
⃝ INSTAGRAM	⃝	⃝
⊕ IG STORIES	⊕	⊕

THURSDAY	FRIDAY	SATURDAY	SUNDAY
f	f	f	f
⊙	⊙	⊙	⊙
⊕	⊕	⊕	⊕

REFLECT & REFINE

f

POST REACH ∧∨ _____

CURRENT # OF FOLLOWERS ∧∨ _____

MOST ENGAGING POST _____

_____

_____

SHARED / ORIGINAL (CIRCLE ONE)

📷

ACCOUNTS REACHED ∧∨ _____

NEW FOLLOWERS _____

CURRENT FOLLOWERS _____

HIGHEST POST REACH:

_____

MOST SAVED CONTENT _____

MOST SHARED CONTENT _____

OF COLLABORATIONS _____

MOST STORY VIEWS _____

BUSINESS RESULTS

OF INVITES SENT? _____

OF CUSTOMERS ENROLLED? _____

INCOME I EARNED? _____

WEEK ENDING

👍 WIN > 🌪 PLOT TWIST

♡ WHY (SELF EVALUATION)

🎯 BIZ GOALS FOR THE WEEK

4 HASH METHOD

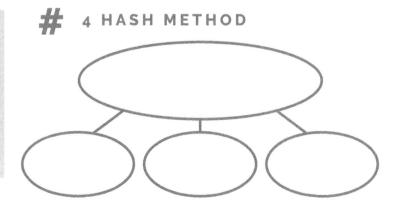

MY INCOME PRODUCING ACTIVITY TRACKER

WEEK OF

			Mon	Tues	Weds	Thur	Fri	Sat	Sun
INCOME PRODUCING ACTIVITIES	**COMMUNITY**	Add Followers							
		Intentional Connect with Followers *not an invite							
		Social Media Post (4 Hash Method)							
		7-10 Stories							
		Highlight People: Testimonials/ Shout Outs							
	CONVERSION	DM people who viewed, liked, commented, or followed							
		Direct invite to service, experience, or product							
		Follow Ups							
	CUSTOMER SERVICE	Ask for Referrals							
		Engage with Current Clients							
		Answer Emails & Messages							
		Business Development							
		Personal Development							

WEEKLY SOCIAL MEDIA PLAN

THINGS TO CONSIDER

- Captions/Taglines
- Content I Like
- Hashtags
- Objections
- Collaborations
- Pain Points
- Well Received Content to Refurbish
- CTA's
- CTT's
- Quotables
- Community Driven Content
- Upcoming Events

CONTENT CREATION CHECKLIST

- ☐ Why are you creating this piece of content?
- ☐ Bold Tagline
- ☐ Personal connection/story
- ☐ Call to Think or Call to Act
- ☐ Image (eye-catching and matches the story)

MONDAY	TUESDAY	WEDNESDAY
f FACEBOOK	f	f
⃝ INSTAGRAM	⃝	⃝
⊕ IG STORIES	⊕	⊕

MY GOAL THIS WEEK:

THURSDAY	FRIDAY	SATURDAY	SUNDAY
f	f	f	f
ⓘ	ⓘ	ⓘ	ⓘ
⊕	⊕	⊕	⊕

REFLECT & REFINE

f

POST REACH ^∨ _____

CURRENT # OF FOLLOWERS ^∨ _____

MOST ENGAGING POST _____

_____

_____

SHARED / ORIGINAL (CIRCLE ONE)

📷

ACCOUNTS REACHED ^∨ _____

NEW FOLLOWERS _____

CURRENT FOLLOWERS _____

HIGHEST POST REACH:

_____

MOST SAVED CONTENT _____

MOST SHARED CONTENT _____

OF COLLABORATIONS _____

MOST STORY VIEWS _____

BUSINESS RESULTS

OF INVITES SENT? _____

OF CUSTOMERS ENROLLED? _____

INCOME I EARNED? _____

WEEK ENDING

👍 WIN > 🌪 PLOT TWIST

♡ WHY (SELF EVALUATION)

🎯 BIZ GOALS FOR THE WEEK

4 HASH METHOD

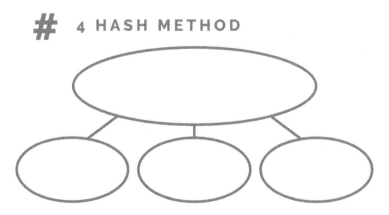

MY INCOME PRODUCING ACTIVITY TRACKER

INCOME PRODUCING ACTIVITIES			Mon	Tues	Weds	Thur	Fri	Sat	Sun
	COMMUNITY	Add Followers							
		Intentional Connect with Followers *not an invite							
		Social Media Post (4 Hash Method)							
		7-10 Stories							
		Highlight People: Testimonials/ Shout Outs							
	CONVERSION	DM people who viewed, liked, commented, or followed							
		Direct invite to service, experience, or product							
		Follow Ups							
	CUSTOMER SERVICE	Ask for Referrals							
		Engage with Current Clients							
		Answer Emails & Messages							
		Business Development							
		Personal Development							

WEEKLY SOCIAL MEDIA PLAN

THINGS TO CONSIDER

- Captions/Taglines
- Content I Like
- Hashtags
- Objections
- Collaborations
- Pain Points
- Well Received Content to Refurbish
- CTA's
- CTT's
- Quotables
- Community Driven Content
- Upcoming Events

CONTENT CREATION CHECKLIST

- ☐ Why are you creating this piece of content?
- ☐ Bold Tagline
- ☐ Personal connection/story
- ☐ Call to Think or Call to Act
- ☐ Image (eye-catching and matches the story)

MONDAY	TUESDAY	WEDNESDAY
f FACEBOOK	**f**	**f**
⃝ INSTAGRAM	⃝	⃝
⊕ IG STORIES	⊕	⊕

THURSDAY	FRIDAY	SATURDAY	SUNDAY
f	f	f	f
◎	◎	◎	◎
⊕	⊕	⊕	⊕

month:

_____

marketing focus:

_____
_____
_____
_____
_____
_____
_____
_____
_____
_____
_____

MONDAY	TUESDAY	WEDNESDAY

MONTHLY GOALS:

THURSDAY	FRIDAY	SATURDAY	SUNDAY

REFLECT & REFINE

f _____

POST REACH $\wedge_\vee$ _____

CURRENT # OF FOLLOWERS $\wedge_\vee$ _____

MOST ENGAGING POST _____

_____

_____

SHARED / ORIGINAL (CIRCLE ONE)

[Instagram] _____

ACCOUNTS REACHED $\wedge_\vee$ _____

NEW FOLLOWERS _____

CURRENT FOLLOWERS _____

HIGHEST POST REACH:

_____

MOST SAVED CONTENT _____

MOST SHARED CONTENT _____

OF COLLABORATIONS _____

MOST STORY VIEWS _____

BUSINESS RESULTS

OF INVITES SENT? _____

OF CUSTOMERS ENROLLED? _____

INCOME I EARNED? _____

WEEK ENDING _____

 WIN > [tornado] PLOT TWIST

[heart] WHY (SELF EVALUATION)

[target] BIZ GOALS FOR THE WEEK

4 HASH METHOD

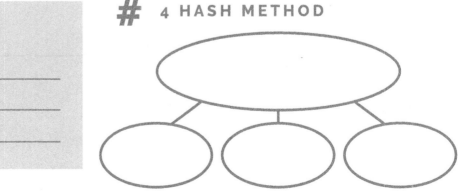

MY INCOME PRODUCING
ACTIVITY TRACKER

			Mon	Tues	Weds	Thur	Fri	Sat	Sun
INCOME PRODUCING ACTIVITIES	**COMMUNITY**	Add Followers							
		Intentional Connect with Followers *not an invite							
		Social Media Post (4 Hash Method)							
		7-10 Stories							
		Highlight People: Testimonials/ Shout Outs							
	CONVERSION	DM people who viewed, liked, commented, or followed							
		Direct invite to service, experience, or product							
		Follow Ups							
	CUSTOMER SERVICE	Ask for Referrals							
		Engage with Current Clients							
		Answer Emails & Messages							
		Business Development							
		Personal Development							

WEEKLY SOCIAL MEDIA PLAN

	MONDAY	TUESDAY	WEDNESDAY
f FACEBOOK	**f**	**f**	
⊙ INSTAGRAM	**⊙**	**⊙**	
⊕ IG STORIES	**⊕**	**⊕**	

THINGS TO CONSIDER

- Captions/Taglines
- Content I Like
- Hashtags
- Objections
- Collaborations
- Pain Points
- Well Received Content to Refurbish
- CTA's
- CTT's
- Quotables
- Community Driven Content
- Upcoming Events

CONTENT CREATION CHECKLIST

- ☐ Why are you creating this piece of content?
- ☐ Bold Tagline
- ☐ Personal connection/story
- ☐ Call to Think or Call to Act
- ☐ Image (eye-catching and matches the story)

THURSDAY	FRIDAY	SATURDAY	SUNDAY
f	f	f	f
◎	◎	◎	◎
⊕	⊕	⊕	⊕

REFLECT & REFINE

f _____

POST REACH ∧∨ _____

CURRENT # OF FOLLOWERS ∧∨ _____

MOST ENGAGING POST _____

_____

_____

SHARED / ORIGINAL (CIRCLE ONE)

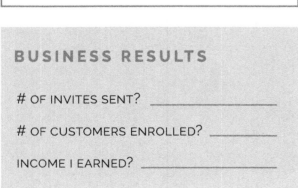

ACCOUNTS REACHED ∧∨ _____

NEW FOLLOWERS _____

CURRENT FOLLOWERS _____

HIGHEST POST REACH:

_____

MOST SAVED CONTENT _____

MOST SHARED CONTENT _____

OF COLLABORATIONS _____

MOST STORY VIEWS _____

BUSINESS RESULTS

OF INVITES SENT? _____

OF CUSTOMERS ENROLLED? _____

INCOME I EARNED? _____

WEEK ENDING

👍 **WIN** > 🌀 **PLOT TWIST**

♡ **WHY (SELF EVALUATION)**

🎯 **BIZ GOALS FOR THE WEEK**

**4 HASH METHOD**

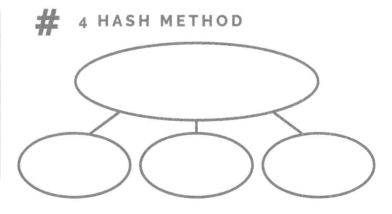

MY INCOME PRODUCING ACTIVITY TRACKER

			Mon	Tues	Weds	Thur	Fri	Sat	Sun
INCOME PRODUCING ACTIVITIES	**COMMUNITY**	Add Followers							
		Intentional Connect with Followers *not an invite							
		Social Media Post (4 Hash Method)							
		7-10 Stories							
		Highlight People: Testimonials/ Shout Outs							
	CONVERSION	DM people who viewed, liked, commented, or followed							
		Direct invite to service, experience, or product							
		Follow Ups							
	CUSTOMER SERVICE	Ask for Referrals							
		Engage with Current Clients							
		Answer Emails & Messages							
		Business Development							
		Personal Development							

WEEKLY SOCIAL MEDIA PLAN

THINGS TO CONSIDER

- Captions/Taglines
- Content I Like
- Hashtags
- Objections
- Collaborations
- Pain Points
- Well Received Content to Refurbish
- CTA's
- CTT's
- Quotables
- Community Driven Content
- Upcoming Events

CONTENT CREATION CHECKLIST

- ☐ Why are you creating this piece of content?
- ☐ Bold Tagline
- ☐ Personal connection/story
- ☐ Call to Think or Call to Act
- ☐ Image (eye-catching and matches the story)

MONDAY	TUESDAY	WEDNESDAY
f FACEBOOK	f	f
⃝ INSTAGRAM	⃝	⃝
⊕ IG STORIES	⊕	⊕

MY GOAL THIS WEEK:

THURSDAY	FRIDAY	SATURDAY	SUNDAY
f	f	f	f
ⓘ	ⓘ	ⓘ	ⓘ
⊕	⊕	⊕	⊕

REFLECT & REFINE

f _____

POST REACH ^∨ _____

CURRENT # OF FOLLOWERS ^∨ _____

MOST ENGAGING POST _____

_____

_____

SHARED / ORIGINAL (CIRCLE ONE)

ACCOUNTS REACHED ^∨ _____

NEW FOLLOWERS _____

CURRENT FOLLOWERS _____

HIGHEST POST REACH:

_____

MOST SAVED CONTENT _____

MOST SHARED CONTENT _____

OF COLLABORATIONS _____

MOST STORY VIEWS _____

BUSINESS RESULTS

OF INVITES SENT? _____

OF CUSTOMERS ENROLLED? _____

INCOME I EARNED? _____

WEEK ENDING

👍 WIN > 🌪 PLOT TWIST

♡ WHY (SELF EVALUATION)

◎ BIZ GOALS FOR THE WEEK

4 HASH METHOD

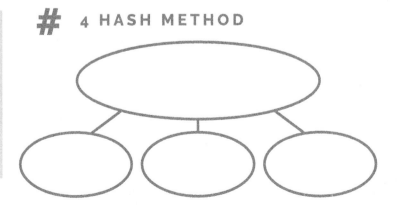

MY INCOME PRODUCING
ACTIVITY TRACKER

		Mon	Tues	Weds	Thur	Fri	Sat	Sun
INCOME PRODUCING ACTIVITIES	**COMMUNITY**	Add Followers						
		Intentional Connect with Followers *not an invite						
		Social Media Post (4 Hash Method)						
		7-10 Stories						
		Highlight People: Testimonials/ Shout Outs						
	CONVERSION	DM people who viewed, liked, commented, or followed						
		Direct invite to service, experience, or product						
		Follow Ups						
	CUSTOMER SERVICE	Ask for Referrals						
		Engage with Current Clients						
		Answer Emails & Messages						
		Business Development						
		Personal Development						

WEEKLY SOCIAL MEDIA PLAN

THINGS TO CONSIDER

- Captions/Taglines
- Content I Like
- Hashtags
- Objections
- Collaborations
- Pain Points
- Well Received Content to Refurbish
- CTA's
- CTT's
- Quotables
- Community Driven Content
- Upcoming Events

CONTENT CREATION CHECKLIST

- ☐ Why are you creating this piece of content?
- ☐ Bold Tagline
- ☐ Personal connection/story
- ☐ Call to Think or Call to Act
- ☐ Image (eye-catching and matches the story)

MONDAY	TUESDAY	WEDNESDAY
f FACEBOOK	f	f
◉ INSTAGRAM	◉	◉
⊕ IG STORIES	⊕	⊕

THURSDAY	FRIDAY	SATURDAY	SUNDAY
f	f	f	f
ⓘ	ⓘ	ⓘ	ⓘ
⊕	⊕	⊕	⊕

REFLECT & REFINE

f

POST REACH ^v _____

CURRENT # OF FOLLOWERS ^v _____

MOST ENGAGING POST _____

_____

_____

SHARED / ORIGINAL (CIRCLE ONE)

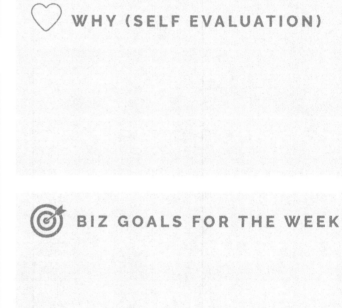

ACCOUNTS REACHED ^v _____

NEW FOLLOWERS _____

CURRENT FOLLOWERS _____

HIGHEST POST REACH:

_____

MOST SAVED CONTENT _____

MOST SHARED CONTENT _____

OF COLLABORATIONS _____

MOST STORY VIEWS _____

WEEK ENDING

👍 WIN > 🌪 PLOT TWIST

♡ WHY (SELF EVALUATION)

🎯 BIZ GOALS FOR THE WEEK

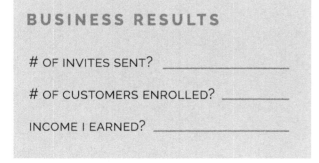

BUSINESS RESULTS

OF INVITES SENT? _____

OF CUSTOMERS ENROLLED? _____

INCOME I EARNED? _____

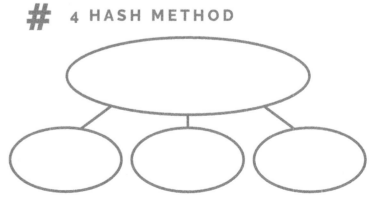

\# 4 HASH METHOD

MY INCOME PRODUCING
ACTIVITY TRACKER

		Mon	Tues	Weds	Thur	Fri	Sat	Sun
INCOME PRODUCING ACTIVITIES	**COMMUNITY**	Add Followers							
		Intentional Connect with Followers *not an invite							
		Social Media Post (4 Hash Method)							
		7-10 Stories							
		Highlight People: Testimonials/ Shout Outs							
	CONVERSION	DM people who viewed, liked, commented, or followed							
		Direct invite to service, experience, or product							
		Follow Ups							
	CUSTOMER SERVICE	Ask for Referrals							
		Engage with Current Clients							
		Answer Emails & Messages							
		Business Development							
		Personal Development							

WEEKLY SOCIAL MEDIA PLAN

THINGS TO CONSIDER

- Captions/Taglines
- Content I Like
- Hashtags
- Objections
- Collaborations
- Pain Points
- Well Received Content to Refurbish
- CTA's
- CTT's
- Quotables
- Community Driven Content
- Upcoming Events

CONTENT CREATION CHECKLIST

- ☐ Why are you creating this piece of content?
- ☐ Bold Tagline
- ☐ Personal connection/story
- ☐ Call to Think or Call to Act
- ☐ Image (eye-catching and matches the story)

MONDAY	TUESDAY	WEDNESDAY
f FACEBOOK	**f**	**f**
⃝ INSTAGRAM	⃝	⃝
⊕ IG STORIES	⊕	⊕

THURSDAY	FRIDAY	SATURDAY	SUNDAY
f	f	f	f
Instagram	Instagram	Instagram	Instagram
⊕	⊕	⊕	⊕

REFLECT & REFINE

f

POST REACH ⌃⌄ _____

CURRENT # OF FOLLOWERS ⌃⌄ _____

MOST ENGAGING POST _____

_____

_____

SHARED / ORIGINAL (CIRCLE ONE)

○

ACCOUNTS REACHED ⌃⌄ _____

NEW FOLLOWERS _____

CURRENT FOLLOWERS _____

HIGHEST POST REACH:

_____

MOST SAVED CONTENT _____

MOST SHARED CONTENT _____

OF COLLABORATIONS _____

MOST STORY VIEWS _____

BUSINESS RESULTS

OF INVITES SENT? _____

OF CUSTOMERS ENROLLED? _____

INCOME I EARNED? _____

_____

WEEK ENDING

👍 WIN > 🌪 PLOT TWIST

♡ WHY (SELF EVALUATION)

🎯 BIZ GOALS FOR THE WEEK

4 HASH METHOD

MY INCOME PRODUCING ACTIVITY TRACKER

		Mon	Tues	Weds	Thur	Fri	Sat	Sun
INCOME PRODUCING ACTIVITIES	**COMMUNITY**	Add Followers						
		Intentional Connect with Followers *not an invite						
		Social Media Post (4 Hash Method)						
		7-10 Stories						
		Highlight People: Testimonials/ Shout Outs						
	CONVERSION	DM people who viewed, liked, commented, or followed						
		Direct invite to service, experience, or product						
		Follow Ups						
	CUSTOMER SERVICE	Ask for Referrals						
		Engage with Current Clients						
		Answer Emails & Messages						
		Business Development						
		Personal Development						

WEEKLY SOCIAL MEDIA PLAN

THINGS TO CONSIDER

- Captions/Taglines
- Content I Like
- Hashtags
- Objections
- Collaborations
- Pain Points
- Well Received Content to Refurbish
- CTA's
- CTT's
- Quotables
- Community Driven Content
- Upcoming Events

CONTENT CREATION CHECKLIST

- ☐ Why are you creating this piece of content?
- ☐ Bold Tagline
- ☐ Personal connection/story
- ☐ Call to Think or Call to Act
- ☐ Image (eye-catching and matches the story)

MONDAY	TUESDAY	WEDNESDAY
f FACEBOOK	**f**	**f**
⃝ INSTAGRAM	⃝	⃝
⊕ IG STORIES	⊕	⊕

THURSDAY	FRIDAY	SATURDAY	SUNDAY
f	f	f	f
Ⓘ	Ⓘ	Ⓘ	Ⓘ
⊕	⊕	⊕	⊕

month:

_____

*marketing
focus:*

_____

_____

_____

_____

_____

_____

_____

_____

_____

_____

MONDAY	TUESDAY	WEDNESDAY

MONTHLY GOALS:

THURSDAY	FRIDAY	SATURDAY	SUNDAY

REFLECT & REFINE

_____
WEEK ENDING

f

POST REACH ∧∨ _____

CURRENT # OF FOLLOWERS ∧∨ _____

MOST ENGAGING POST _____

_____

_____

SHARED / ORIGINAL (CIRCLE ONE)

WIN > 🌪 PLOT TWIST

♡ WHY (SELF EVALUATION)

📷

ACCOUNTS REACHED ∧∨ _____

NEW FOLLOWERS _____

CURRENT FOLLOWERS _____

HIGHEST POST REACH:

_____

MOST SAVED CONTENT _____

MOST SHARED CONTENT _____

OF COLLABORATIONS _____

MOST STORY VIEWS _____

🎯 BIZ GOALS FOR THE WEEK

BUSINESS RESULTS

OF INVITES SENT? _____

OF CUSTOMERS ENROLLED? _____

INCOME I EARNED? _____

4 HASH METHOD

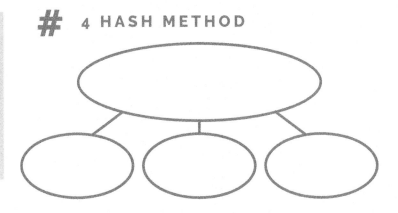

MY INCOME PRODUCING ACTIVITY TRACKER

WEEK OF

			Mon	Tues	Weds	Thur	Fri	Sat	Sun
INCOME PRODUCING ACTIVITIES	**COMMUNITY**	Add Followers							
		Intentional Connect with Followers *not an invite							
		Social Media Post (4 Hash Method)							
		7-10 Stories							
		Highlight People: Testimonials/ Shout Outs							
	CONVERSION	DM people who viewed, liked, commented, or followed							
		Direct invite to service, experience, or product							
		Follow Ups							
	CUSTOMER SERVICE	Ask for Referrals							
		Engage with Current Clients							
		Answer Emails & Messages							
		Business Development							
		Personal Development							

WEEKLY SOCIAL MEDIA PLAN

THINGS TO CONSIDER

- Captions/Taglines
- Content I Like
- Hashtags
- Objections
- Collaborations
- Pain Points
- Well Received Content to Refurbish
- CTA's
- CTT's
- Quotables
- Community Driven Content
- Upcoming Events

CONTENT CREATION CHECKLIST

- ☐ Why are you creating this piece of content?
- ☐ Bold Tagline
- ☐ Personal connection/story
- ☐ Call to Think or Call to Act
- ☐ Image (eye-catching and matches the story)

MONDAY	TUESDAY	WEDNESDAY
f FACEBOOK	**f**	**f**
⃝ INSTAGRAM	⃝	⃝
⊕ IG STORIES	⊕	⊕

THURSDAY	FRIDAY	SATURDAY	SUNDAY
f	f	f	f
⊙	⊙	⊙	⊙
⊕	⊕	⊕	⊕

REFLECT & REFINE

f

POST REACH ∧∨ _____

CURRENT # OF FOLLOWERS ∧∨ _____

MOST ENGAGING POST _____

_____

_____

SHARED / ORIGINAL (CIRCLE ONE)

👍 WIN > 🌪 PLOT TWIST

♡ WHY (SELF EVALUATION)

📷

ACCOUNTS REACHED ∧∨ _____

NEW FOLLOWERS _____

CURRENT FOLLOWERS _____

HIGHEST POST REACH:

_____

MOST SAVED CONTENT _____

MOST SHARED CONTENT _____

OF COLLABORATIONS _____

MOST STORY VIEWS _____

🎯 BIZ GOALS FOR THE WEEK

BUSINESS RESULTS

OF INVITES SENT? _____

OF CUSTOMERS ENROLLED? _____

INCOME I EARNED? _____

4 HASH METHOD

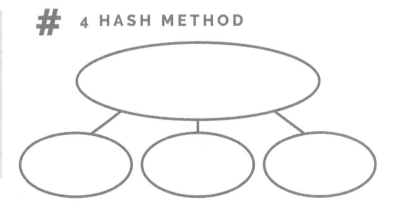

MY INCOME PRODUCING ACTIVITY TRACKER

WEEK OF _____

INCOME PRODUCING ACTIVITIES			Mon	Tues	Weds	Thur	Fri	Sat	Sun
	COMMUNITY	Add Followers							
		Intentional Connect with Followers *not an invite							
		Social Media Post (4 Hash Method)							
		7-10 Stories							
		Highlight People: Testimonials/ Shout Outs							
	CONVERSION	DM people who viewed, liked, commented, or followed							
		Direct invite to service, experience, or product							
		Follow Ups							
	CUSTOMER SERVICE	Ask for Referrals							
		Engage with Current Clients							
		Answer Emails & Messages							
		Business Development							
		Personal Development							

WEEKLY SOCIAL MEDIA PLAN

THINGS TO CONSIDER

- Captions/Taglines
- Content I Like
- Hashtags
- Objections
- Collaborations
- Pain Points
- Well Received Content to Refurbish
- CTA's
- CTT's
- Quotables
- Community Driven Content
- Upcoming Events

CONTENT CREATION CHECKLIST

- ☐ Why are you creating this piece of content?
- ☐ Bold Tagline
- ☐ Personal connection/story
- ☐ Call to Think or Call to Act
- ☐ Image (eye-catching and matches the story)

MONDAY	TUESDAY	WEDNESDAY
f FACEBOOK	**f**	**f**
⊙ INSTAGRAM	⊙	⊙
⊕ IG STORIES	⊕	⊕

THURSDAY	FRIDAY	SATURDAY	SUNDAY
f	f	f	f
ⓘ	ⓘ	ⓘ	ⓘ
⊕	⊕	⊕	⊕

REFLECT & REFINE

f

POST REACH ^∨ _____

CURRENT # OF FOLLOWERS ^∨ _____

MOST ENGAGING POST _____

_____

_____

SHARED / ORIGINAL (CIRCLE ONE)

Instagram

ACCOUNTS REACHED ^∨ _____

NEW FOLLOWERS _____

CURRENT FOLLOWERS _____

HIGHEST POST REACH:

_____

MOST SAVED CONTENT _____

MOST SHARED CONTENT _____

OF COLLABORATIONS _____

MOST STORY VIEWS _____

BUSINESS RESULTS

OF INVITES SENT? _____

OF CUSTOMERS ENROLLED? _____

INCOME I EARNED? _____

WEEK ENDING

👍 WIN > 🌪 PLOT TWIST

♡ WHY (SELF EVALUATION)

🎯 BIZ GOALS FOR THE WEEK

\# 4 HASH METHOD

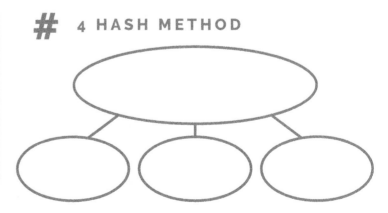

MY INCOME PRODUCING
ACTIVITY TRACKER

		Mon	Tues	Weds	Thur	Fri	Sat	Sun
INCOME PRODUCING ACTIVITIES	**COMMUNITY**	Add Followers						
		Intentional Connect with Followers *not an invite						
		Social Media Post (4 Hash Method)						
		7-10 Stories						
		Highlight People: Testimonials/ Shout Outs						
	CONVERSION	DM people who viewed, liked, commented, or followed						
		Direct invite to service, experience, or product						
		Follow Ups						
	CUSTOMER SERVICE	Ask for Referrals						
		Engage with Current Clients						
		Answer Emails & Messages						
		Business Development						
		Personal Development						

WEEKLY SOCIAL MEDIA PLAN

THINGS TO CONSIDER

- Captions/Taglines
- Content I Like
- Hashtags
- Objections
- Collaborations
- Pain Points
- Well Received Content to Refurbish
- CTA's
- CTT's
- Quotables
- Community Driven Content
- Upcoming Events

CONTENT CREATION CHECKLIST

- ☐ Why are you creating this piece of content?
- ☐ Bold Tagline
- ☐ Personal connection/story
- ☐ Call to Think or Call to Act
- ☐ Image (eye-catching and matches the story)

MONDAY	TUESDAY	WEDNESDAY
f FACEBOOK	**f**	**f**
INSTAGRAM		
IG STORIES		

MY GOAL THIS WEEK:

THURSDAY	FRIDAY	SATURDAY	SUNDAY
f	f	f	f
⊙	⊙	⊙	⊙
⊕	⊕	⊕	⊕

REFLECT & REFINE

f _____

POST REACH $\wedge\atop\vee$ _____

CURRENT # OF FOLLOWERS $\wedge\atop\vee$ _____

MOST ENGAGING POST _____

_____

_____

SHARED / ORIGINAL (CIRCLE ONE)

⊙ _____

ACCOUNTS REACHED $\wedge\atop\vee$ _____

NEW FOLLOWERS _____

CURRENT FOLLOWERS _____

HIGHEST POST REACH:

_____

MOST SAVED CONTENT _____

MOST SHARED CONTENT _____

OF COLLABORATIONS _____

MOST STORY VIEWS _____

BUSINESS RESULTS

OF INVITES SENT? _____

OF CUSTOMERS ENROLLED? _____

INCOME I EARNED? _____

WEEK ENDING

👍 WIN > 🌪 PLOT TWIST

♡ WHY (SELF EVALUATION)

◎ BIZ GOALS FOR THE WEEK

\# 4 HASH METHOD

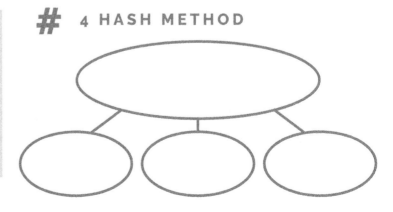

MY INCOME PRODUCING
ACTIVITY TRACKER

		Mon	Tues	Weds	Thur	Fri	Sat	Sun
INCOME PRODUCING ACTIVITIES	**COMMUNITY**	Add Followers							
		Intentional Connect with Followers *not an invite							
		Social Media Post (4 Hash Method)							
		7-10 Stories							
		Highlight People: Testimonials/ Shout Outs							
	CONVERSION	DM people who viewed, liked, commented, or followed							
		Direct invite to service, experience, or product							
		Follow Ups							
	CUSTOMER SERVICE	Ask for Referrals							
		Engage with Current Clients							
		Answer Emails & Messages							
		Business Development							
		Personal Development							

WEEKLY SOCIAL MEDIA PLAN

THINGS TO CONSIDER

- Captions/Taglines
- Content I Like
- Hashtags
- Objections
- Collaborations
- Pain Points
- Well Received Content to Refurbish
- CTA's
- CTT's
- Quotables
- Community Driven Content
- Upcoming Events

CONTENT CREATION CHECKLIST

- [ ] Why are you creating this piece of content?
- [ ] Bold Tagline
- [ ] Personal connection/story
- [ ] Call to Think or Call to Act
- [ ] Image (eye-catching and matches the story)

MONDAY	TUESDAY	WEDNESDAY
f FACEBOOK	**f**	**f**
⦿ INSTAGRAM	⦿	⦿
⊕ IG STORIES	⊕	⊕

MY GOAL THIS WEEK:

THURSDAY	FRIDAY	SATURDAY	SUNDAY
f	f	f	f
⃝	⃝	⃝	⃝
⊕	⊕	⊕	⊕

REFLECT & REFINE

f

POST REACH ︿﹀ _____

CURRENT # OF FOLLOWERS ︿﹀ _____

MOST ENGAGING POST _____

_____

_____

SHARED / ORIGINAL (CIRCLE ONE)

⊙

ACCOUNTS REACHED ︿﹀ _____

NEW FOLLOWERS _____

CURRENT FOLLOWERS _____

HIGHEST POST REACH:

_____

MOST SAVED CONTENT _____

MOST SHARED CONTENT _____

OF COLLABORATIONS _____

MOST STORY VIEWS _____

BUSINESS RESULTS

OF INVITES SENT? _____

OF CUSTOMERS ENROLLED? _____

INCOME I EARNED? _____

_____

WEEK ENDING

👍 WIN > 🌀 PLOT TWIST

♡ WHY (SELF EVALUATION)

🎯 BIZ GOALS FOR THE WEEK

4 HASH METHOD

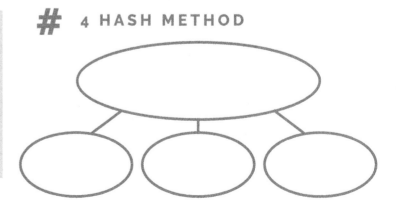

MY INCOME PRODUCING
ACTIVITY TRACKER

			Mon	Tues	Weds	Thur	Fri	Sat	Sun
INCOME PRODUCING ACTIVITIES	**COMMUNITY**	Add Followers							
		Intentional Connect with Followers *not an invite							
		Social Media Post (4 Hash Method)							
		7-10 Stories							
		Highlight People: Testimonials/ Shout Outs							
	CONVERSION	DM people who viewed, liked, commented, or followed							
		Direct invite to service, experience, or product							
		Follow Ups							
	CUSTOMER SERVICE	Ask for Referrals							
		Engage with Current Clients							
		Answer Emails & Messages							
		Business Development							
		Personal Development							

WEEKLY SOCIAL MEDIA PLAN

THINGS TO CONSIDER

- Captions/Taglines
- Content I Like
- Hashtags
- Objections
- Collaborations
- Pain Points
- Well Received Content to Refurbish
- CTA's
- CTT's
- Quotables
- Community Driven Content
- Upcoming Events

CONTENT CREATION CHECKLIST

- ☐ Why are you creating this piece of content?
- ☐ Bold Tagline
- ☐ Personal connection/story
- ☐ Call to Think or Call to Act
- ☐ Image (eye-catching and matches the story)

MONDAY	TUESDAY	WEDNESDAY
f FACEBOOK	**f**	**f**
⃝ INSTAGRAM	⃝	⃝
⊕ IG STORIES	⊕	⊕

MY GOAL THIS WEEK:

THURSDAY	FRIDAY	SATURDAY	SUNDAY
f	f	f	f
⊙	⊙	⊙	⊙
⊕	⊕	⊕	⊕

month:

_____

*marketing
focus:*

_____

_____

_____

_____

_____

_____

_____

_____

_____

_____

_____

MONDAY	TUESDAY	WEDNESDAY

MONTHLY GOALS:

THURSDAY	FRIDAY	SATURDAY	SUNDAY

REFLECT & REFINE

f

POST REACH ^v _____

CURRENT # OF FOLLOWERS ^v _____

MOST ENGAGING POST _____

_____

_____

SHARED / ORIGINAL (CIRCLE ONE)

Instagram

ACCOUNTS REACHED ^v _____

NEW FOLLOWERS _____

CURRENT FOLLOWERS _____

HIGHEST POST REACH:

_____

MOST SAVED CONTENT _____

MOST SHARED CONTENT _____

OF COLLABORATIONS _____

MOST STORY VIEWS _____

BUSINESS RESULTS

OF INVITES SENT? _____

OF CUSTOMERS ENROLLED? _____

INCOME I EARNED? _____

WEEK ENDING _____

👍 WIN > 🌪 PLOT TWIST

♡ WHY (SELF EVALUATION)

🎯 BIZ GOALS FOR THE WEEK

4 HASH METHOD

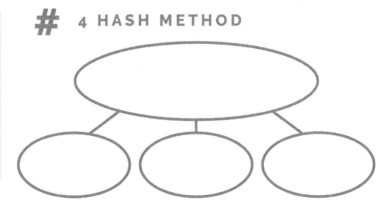

MY INCOME PRODUCING
ACTIVITY TRACKER

		Mon	Tues	Weds	Thur	Fri	Sat	Sun
INCOME PRODUCING ACTIVITIES	**COMMUNITY**	Add Followers							
		Intentional Connect with Followers *not an invite							
		Social Media Post (4 Hash Method)							
		7-10 Stories							
		Highlight People: Testimonials/ Shout Outs							
	CONVERSION	DM people who viewed, liked, commented, or followed							
		Direct invite to service, experience, or product							
		Follow Ups							
	CUSTOMER SERVICE	Ask for Referrals							
		Engage with Current Clients							
		Answer Emails & Messages							
		Business Development							
		Personal Development							

WEEKLY SOCIAL MEDIA PLAN

THINGS TO CONSIDER

- Captions/Taglines
- Content I Like
- Hashtags
- Objections
- Collaborations
- Pain Points
- Well Received Content to Refurbish
- CTA's
- CTT's
- Quotables
- Community Driven Content
- Upcoming Events

CONTENT CREATION CHECKLIST

- ☐ Why are you creating this piece of content?
- ☐ Bold Tagline
- ☐ Personal connection/story
- ☐ Call to Think or Call to Act
- ☐ Image (eye-catching and matches the story)

MONDAY	TUESDAY	WEDNESDAY
f FACEBOOK	f	f
⃝ INSTAGRAM	⃝	⃝
⊕ IG STORIES	⊕	⊕

THURSDAY	FRIDAY	SATURDAY	SUNDAY
f	f	f	f
ⓘ	ⓘ	ⓘ	ⓘ
⊕	⊕	⊕	⊕

REFLECT & REFINE

f

POST REACH ^v _____

CURRENT # OF FOLLOWERS ^v _____

MOST ENGAGING POST _____

_____

_____

SHARED / ORIGINAL (CIRCLE ONE)

WEEK ENDING

👍 WIN > 🌪 PLOT TWIST

♡ WHY (SELF EVALUATION)

🎯 BIZ GOALS FOR THE WEEK

📷

ACCOUNTS REACHED ^v _____

NEW FOLLOWERS _____

CURRENT FOLLOWERS _____

HIGHEST POST REACH:

_____

MOST SAVED CONTENT _____

MOST SHARED CONTENT _____

OF COLLABORATIONS _____

MOST STORY VIEWS _____

BUSINESS RESULTS

OF INVITES SENT? _____

OF CUSTOMERS ENROLLED? _____

INCOME I EARNED? _____

4 HASH METHOD

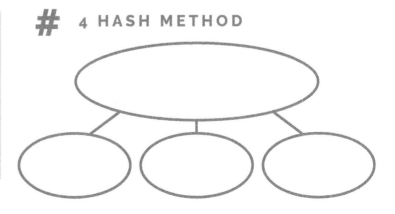

MY INCOME PRODUCING ACTIVITY TRACKER

		Mon	Tues	Weds	Thur	Fri	Sat	Sun
INCOME PRODUCING ACTIVITIES	**COMMUNITY**	Add Followers						
		Intentional Connect with Followers *not an invite						
		Social Media Post (4 Hash Method)						
		7-10 Stories						
		Highlight People: Testimonials/ Shout Outs						
	CONVERSION	DM people who viewed, liked, commented, or followed						
		Direct invite to service, experience, or product						
		Follow Ups						
	CUSTOMER SERVICE	Ask for Referrals						
		Engage with Current Clients						
		Answer Emails & Messages						
		Business Development						
		Personal Development						

WEEKLY SOCIAL MEDIA PLAN

THINGS TO CONSIDER

- Captions/Taglines
- Content I Like
- Hashtags
- Objections
- Collaborations
- Pain Points
- Well Received Content to Refurbish
- CTA's
- CTT's
- Quotables
- Community Driven Content
- Upcoming Events

CONTENT CREATION CHECKLIST

- ☐ Why are you creating this piece of content?
- ☐ Bold Tagline
- ☐ Personal connection/story
- ☐ Call to Think or Call to Act
- ☐ Image (eye-catching and matches the story)

MONDAY	TUESDAY	WEDNESDAY
f FACEBOOK	**f**	**f**
⊙ INSTAGRAM	⊙	⊙
⊕ IG STORIES	⊕	⊕

THURSDAY	FRIDAY	SATURDAY	SUNDAY
f	f	f	f
⬛	⬛	⬛	⬛
⊕	⊕	⊕	⊕

REFLECT & REFINE

f

POST REACH ^v _____

CURRENT # OF FOLLOWERS ^v _____

MOST ENGAGING POST _____

_____

_____

SHARED / ORIGINAL (CIRCLE ONE)

(Instagram)

ACCOUNTS REACHED ^v _____

NEW FOLLOWERS _____

CURRENT FOLLOWERS _____

HIGHEST POST REACH:

_____

MOST SAVED CONTENT _____

MOST SHARED CONTENT _____

OF COLLABORATIONS _____

MOST STORY VIEWS _____

BUSINESS RESULTS

OF INVITES SENT? _____

OF CUSTOMERS ENROLLED? _____

INCOME I EARNED? _____

_____

WEEK ENDING

👍 WIN > 🌪 PLOT TWIST

♡ WHY (SELF EVALUATION)

🎯 BIZ GOALS FOR THE WEEK

4 HASH METHOD

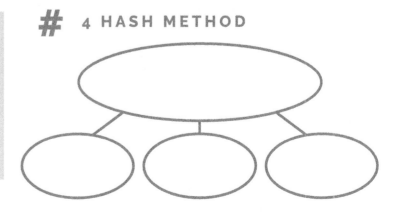

MY INCOME PRODUCING
ACTIVITY TRACKER

		Mon	Tues	Weds	Thur	Fri	Sat	Sun
INCOME PRODUCING ACTIVITIES	**COMMUNITY**	Add Followers						
		Intentional Connect with Followers *not an invite						
		Social Media Post (4 Hash Method)						
		7-10 Stories						
		Highlight People: Testimonials/ Shout Outs						
	CONVERSION	DM people who viewed, liked, commented, or followed						
		Direct invite to service, experience, or product						
		Follow Ups						
	CUSTOMER SERVICE	Ask for Referrals						
		Engage with Current Clients						
		Answer Emails & Messages						
		Business Development						
		Personal Development						

WEEKLY SOCIAL MEDIA PLAN

THINGS TO CONSIDER

- Captions/Taglines
- Content I Like
- Hashtags
- Objections
- Collaborations
- Pain Points
- Well Received Content to Refurbish
- CTA's
- CTT's
- Quotables
- Community Driven Content
- Upcoming Events

CONTENT CREATION CHECKLIST

- ☐ Why are you creating this piece of content?
- ☐ Bold Tagline
- ☐ Personal connection/story
- ☐ Call to Think or Call to Act
- ☐ Image (eye-catching and matches the story)

MONDAY	TUESDAY	WEDNESDAY
f FACEBOOK	f	f
ⓘ INSTAGRAM	ⓘ	ⓘ
⊕ IG STORIES	⊕	⊕

THURSDAY	FRIDAY	SATURDAY	SUNDAY
f	f	f	f
[o]	[o]	[o]	[o]
(+)	(+)	(+)	(+)

REFLECT & REFINE

f _____

POST REACH ∧∨ _____

CURRENT # OF FOLLOWERS ∧∨ _____

MOST ENGAGING POST _____

_____

_____

SHARED / ORIGINAL (CIRCLE ONE)

📷 _____

ACCOUNTS REACHED ∧∨ _____

NEW FOLLOWERS _____

CURRENT FOLLOWERS _____

HIGHEST POST REACH:

_____

MOST SAVED CONTENT _____

MOST SHARED CONTENT _____

OF COLLABORATIONS _____

MOST STORY VIEWS _____

BUSINESS RESULTS

OF INVITES SENT? _____

OF CUSTOMERS ENROLLED? _____

INCOME I EARNED? _____

WEEK ENDING

👍 **WIN >** 🌪 **PLOT TWIST**

♡ **WHY (SELF EVALUATION)**

🎯 **BIZ GOALS FOR THE WEEK**

4 HASH METHOD

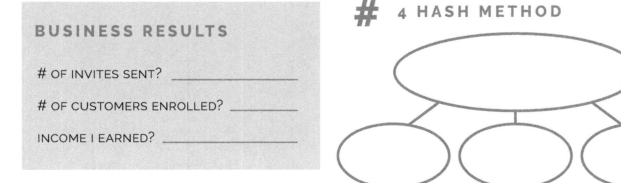

MY INCOME PRODUCING
ACTIVITY TRACKER

		Mon	Tues	Weds	Thur	Fri	Sat	Sun
INCOME PRODUCING ACTIVITIES	**COMMUNITY**	Add Followers						
		Intentional Connect with Followers *not an invite						
		Social Media Post (4 Hash Method)						
		7-10 Stories						
		Highlight People: Testimonials/ Shout Outs						
	CONVERSION	DM people who viewed, liked, commented, or followed						
		Direct invite to service, experience, or product						
		Follow Ups						
	CUSTOMER SERVICE	Ask for Referrals						
		Engage with Current Clients						
		Answer Emails & Messages						
		Business Development						
		Personal Development						

WEEKLY SOCIAL MEDIA PLAN

THINGS TO CONSIDER

- Captions/Taglines
- Content I Like
- Hashtags
- Objections
- Collaborations
- Pain Points
- Well Received Content to Refurbish
- CTA's
- CTT's
- Quotables
- Community Driven Content
- Upcoming Events

CONTENT CREATION CHECKLIST

- ☐ Why are you creating this piece of content?
- ☐ Bold Tagline
- ☐ Personal connection/story
- ☐ Call to Think or Call to Act
- ☐ Image (eye-catching and matches the story)

MONDAY	TUESDAY	WEDNESDAY
f FACEBOOK	f	f
◉ INSTAGRAM	◉	◉
⊕ IG STORIES	⊕	⊕

MY GOAL THIS WEEK:

THURSDAY	FRIDAY	SATURDAY	SUNDAY
f	f	f	f
◉	◉	◉	◉
⊕	⊕	⊕	⊕

REFLECT & REFINE

f

POST REACH ∧∨ _____

CURRENT # OF FOLLOWERS ∧∨ _____

MOST ENGAGING POST _____

_____

_____

SHARED / ORIGINAL (CIRCLE ONE)

ACCOUNTS REACHED ∧∨ _____

NEW FOLLOWERS _____

CURRENT FOLLOWERS _____

HIGHEST POST REACH:

_____

MOST SAVED CONTENT _____

MOST SHARED CONTENT _____

OF COLLABORATIONS _____

MOST STORY VIEWS _____

BUSINESS RESULTS

OF INVITES SENT? _____

OF CUSTOMERS ENROLLED? _____

INCOME I EARNED? _____

👍 WIN > 🌪 PLOT TWIST

♡ WHY (SELF EVALUATION)

🎯 BIZ GOALS FOR THE WEEK

4 HASH METHOD

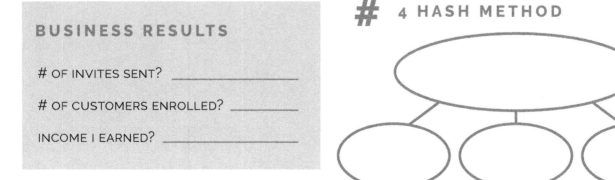

MY INCOME PRODUCING ACTIVITY TRACKER

INCOME PRODUCING ACTIVITIES			Mon	Tues	Weds	Thur	Fri	Sat	Sun
	COMMUNITY	Add Followers							
		Intentional Connect with Followers *not an invite							
		Social Media Post (4 Hash Method)							
		7-10 Stories							
		Highlight People: Testimonials/ Shout Outs							
	CONVERSION	DM people who viewed, liked, commented, or followed							
		Direct invite to service, experience, or product							
		Follow Ups							
	CUSTOMER SERVICE	Ask for Referrals							
		Engage with Current Clients							
		Answer Emails & Messages							
		Business Development							
		Personal Development							

WEEKLY SOCIAL MEDIA PLAN

THINGS TO CONSIDER

- Captions/Taglines
- Content I Like
- Hashtags
- Objections
- Collaborations
- Pain Points
- Well Received Content to Refurbish
- CTA's
- CTT's
- Quotables
- Community Driven Content
- Upcoming Events

CONTENT CREATION CHECKLIST

- ☐ Why are you creating this piece of content?
- ☐ Bold Tagline
- ☐ Personal connection/story
- ☐ Call to Think or Call to Act
- ☐ Image (eye-catching and matches the story)

MONDAY	TUESDAY	WEDNESDAY
f FACEBOOK	**f**	**f**
⭘ INSTAGRAM	⭘	⭘
⊕ IG STORIES	⊕	⊕

THURSDAY	FRIDAY	SATURDAY	SUNDAY
f	f	f	f
ⓘ	ⓘ	ⓘ	ⓘ
⊕	⊕	⊕	⊕

month:

_____

marketing focus:

_____
_____
_____
_____
_____
_____
_____
_____
_____
_____
_____
_____

MONDAY	TUESDAY	WEDNESDAY

MONTHLY GOALS:

THURSDAY	FRIDAY	SATURDAY	SUNDAY

REFLECT & REFINE

f

POST REACH ∧∨ _____

CURRENT # OF FOLLOWERS ∧∨ _____

MOST ENGAGING POST _____

_____

_____

SHARED / ORIGINAL (CIRCLE ONE)

ACCOUNTS REACHED ∧∨ _____

NEW FOLLOWERS _____

CURRENT FOLLOWERS _____

HIGHEST POST REACH:

_____

MOST SAVED CONTENT _____

MOST SHARED CONTENT _____

OF COLLABORATIONS _____

MOST STORY VIEWS _____

BUSINESS RESULTS

OF INVITES SENT? _____

OF CUSTOMERS ENROLLED? _____

INCOME I EARNED? _____

👍 WIN > 🌪 PLOT TWIST

♡ WHY (SELF EVALUATION)

🎯 BIZ GOALS FOR THE WEEK

\# 4 HASH METHOD

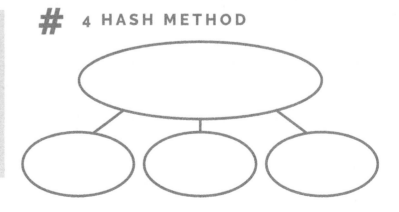

MY INCOME PRODUCING ACTIVITY TRACKER

WEEK OF

		Mon	Tues	Weds	Thur	Fri	Sat	Sun
INCOME PRODUCING ACTIVITIES	**COMMUNITY**	Add Followers							
		Intentional Connect with Followers *not an invite							
		Social Media Post (4 Hash Method)							
		7-10 Stories							
		Highlight People: Testimonials/ Shout Outs							
	CONVERSION	DM people who viewed, liked, commented, or followed							
		Direct invite to service, experience, or product							
		Follow Ups							
	CUSTOMER SERVICE	Ask for Referrals							
		Engage with Current Clients							
		Answer Emails & Messages							
		Business Development							
		Personal Development							

WEEKLY SOCIAL MEDIA PLAN

THINGS TO CONSIDER

- Captions/Taglines
- Content I Like
- Hashtags
- Objections
- Collaborations
- Pain Points
- Well Received
  Content to Refurbish
- CTA's
- CTT's
- Quotables
- Community Driven
  Content
- Upcoming Events

CONTENT CREATION CHECKLIST

- ☐ Why are you creating this piece of content?

- ☐ Bold Tagline

- ☐ Personal connection/story

- ☐ Call to Think or Call to Act

- ☐ Image (eye-catching and matches the story)

MONDAY	TUESDAY	WEDNESDAY
f FACEBOOK	**f**	**f**
⊙ INSTAGRAM	⊙	⊙
⊕ IG STORIES	⊕	⊕

THURSDAY	FRIDAY	SATURDAY	SUNDAY
f	f	f	f
⃝	⃝	⃝	⃝
⊕	⊕	⊕	⊕

REFLECT & REFINE

f

POST REACH ⌃⌄ _____

CURRENT # OF FOLLOWERS ⌃⌄ _____

MOST ENGAGING POST _____

_____

_____

SHARED / ORIGINAL (CIRCLE ONE)

⦿

ACCOUNTS REACHED ⌃⌄ _____

NEW FOLLOWERS _____

CURRENT FOLLOWERS _____

HIGHEST POST REACH:

_____

MOST SAVED CONTENT _____

MOST SHARED CONTENT _____

OF COLLABORATIONS _____

MOST STORY VIEWS _____

BUSINESS RESULTS

OF INVITES SENT? _____

OF CUSTOMERS ENROLLED? _____

INCOME I EARNED? _____

WEEK ENDING

👍 WIN > 🌀 PLOT TWIST

♡ WHY (SELF EVALUATION)

◎ BIZ GOALS FOR THE WEEK

4 HASH METHOD

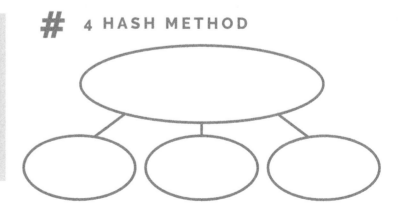

MY INCOME PRODUCING ACTIVITY TRACKER

INCOME PRODUCING ACTIVITIES			Mon	Tues	Weds	Thur	Fri	Sat	Sun
	COMMUNITY	Add Followers							
		Intentional Connect with Followers *not an invite							
		Social Media Post (4 Hash Method)							
		7-10 Stories							
		Highlight People: Testimonials/ Shout Outs							
	CONVERSION	DM people who viewed, liked, commented, or followed							
		Direct invite to service, experience, or product							
		Follow Ups							
	CUSTOMER SERVICE	Ask for Referrals							
		Engage with Current Clients							
		Answer Emails & Messages							
		Business Development							
		Personal Development							

WEEKLY SOCIAL MEDIA PLAN

THINGS TO CONSIDER

- Captions/Taglines
- Content I Like
- Hashtags
- Objections
- Collaborations
- Pain Points
- Well Received
  Content to Refurbish
- CTA's
- CTT's
- Quotables
- Community Driven
  Content
- Upcoming Events

CONTENT CREATION CHECKLIST

- [ ] Why are you creating this piece of content?
- [ ] Bold Tagline
- [ ] Personal connection/story
- [ ] Call to Think or Call to Act
- [ ] Image (eye-catching and matches the story)

	MONDAY	TUESDAY	WEDNESDAY
FACEBOOK	f	f	f
INSTAGRAM	⊙	⊙	⊙
IG STORIES	⊕	⊕	⊕

THURSDAY	FRIDAY	SATURDAY	SUNDAY
f	f	f	f
⃝	⃝	⃝	⃝
⊕	⊕	⊕	⊕

REFLECT & REFINE

f

POST REACH ^v _____

CURRENT # OF FOLLOWERS ^v _____

MOST ENGAGING POST _____

_____

_____

SHARED / ORIGINAL (CIRCLE ONE)

ACCOUNTS REACHED ^v _____

NEW FOLLOWERS _____

CURRENT FOLLOWERS _____

HIGHEST POST REACH:

_____

MOST SAVED CONTENT _____

MOST SHARED CONTENT _____

OF COLLABORATIONS _____

MOST STORY VIEWS _____

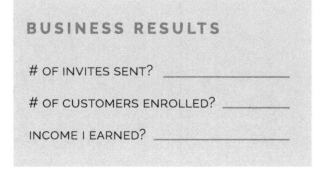

BUSINESS RESULTS

OF INVITES SENT? _____

OF CUSTOMERS ENROLLED? _____

INCOME I EARNED? _____

_____

WEEK ENDING

👍 WIN > 🌀 PLOT TWIST

♡ WHY (SELF EVALUATION)

◎ BIZ GOALS FOR THE WEEK

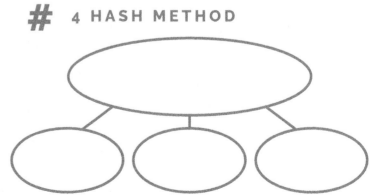

\# 4 HASH METHOD

MY INCOME PRODUCING
ACTIVITY TRACKER

WEEK OF

		Mon	Tues	Weds	Thur	Fri	Sat	Sun
INCOME PRODUCING ACTIVITIES	**COMMUNITY**							
		Add Followers						
		Intentional Connect with Followers *not an invite						
		Social Media Post (4 Hash Method)						
		7-10 Stories						
		Highlight People: Testimonials/ Shout Outs						
	CONVERSION	DM people who viewed, liked, commented, or followed						
		Direct invite to service, experience, or product						
		Follow Ups						
	CUSTOMER SERVICE	Ask for Referrals						
		Engage with Current Clients						
		Answer Emails & Messages						
		Business Development						
		Personal Development						

WEEKLY SOCIAL MEDIA PLAN

THINGS TO CONSIDER

- Captions/Taglines
- Content I Like
- Hashtags
- Objections
- Collaborations
- Pain Points
- Well Received Content to Refurbish
- CTA's
- CTT's
- Quotables
- Community Driven Content
- Upcoming Events

CONTENT CREATION CHECKLIST

- ☐ Why are you creating this piece of content?
- ☐ Bold Tagline
- ☐ Personal connection/story
- ☐ Call to Think or Call to Act
- ☐ Image (eye-catching and matches the story)

MONDAY	TUESDAY	WEDNESDAY
f FACEBOOK	**f**	**f**
⃝ INSTAGRAM	⃝	⃝
⊕ IG STORIES	⊕	⊕

THURSDAY	FRIDAY	SATURDAY	SUNDAY
f	f	f	f
ⓘ	ⓘ	ⓘ	ⓘ
⊕	⊕	⊕	⊕

REFLECT & REFINE

f

POST REACH ∧∨ _____

CURRENT # OF FOLLOWERS ∧∨ _____

MOST ENGAGING POST _____

_____

_____

SHARED / ORIGINAL (CIRCLE ONE)

⊙

ACCOUNTS REACHED ∧∨ _____

NEW FOLLOWERS _____

CURRENT FOLLOWERS _____

HIGHEST POST REACH:

_____

MOST SAVED CONTENT _____

MOST SHARED CONTENT _____

OF COLLABORATIONS _____

MOST STORY VIEWS _____

BUSINESS RESULTS

OF INVITES SENT? _____

OF CUSTOMERS ENROLLED? _____

INCOME I EARNED? _____

_____
WEEK ENDING

👍 WIN > 🌪 PLOT TWIST

♡ WHY (SELF EVALUATION)

◎ BIZ GOALS FOR THE WEEK

4 HASH METHOD

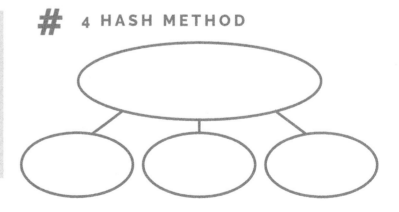

MY INCOME PRODUCING ACTIVITY TRACKER

		Mon	Tues	Weds	Thur	Fri	Sat	Sun
INCOME PRODUCING ACTIVITIES	**COMMUNITY**	Add Followers						
		Intentional Connect with Followers *not an invite						
		Social Media Post (4 Hash Method)						
		7-10 Stories						
		Highlight People: Testimonials/ Shout Outs						
	CONVERSION	DM people who viewed, liked, commented, or followed						
		Direct invite to service, experience, or product						
		Follow Ups						
	CUSTOMER SERVICE	Ask for Referrals						
		Engage with Current Clients						
		Answer Emails & Messages						
		Business Development						
		Personal Development						

WEEKLY SOCIAL MEDIA PLAN

THINGS TO CONSIDER

- Captions/Taglines
- Content I Like
- Hashtags
- Objections
- Collaborations
- Pain Points
- Well Received Content to Refurbish
- CTA's
- CTT's
- Quotables
- Community Driven Content
- Upcoming Events

CONTENT CREATION CHECKLIST

- ☐ Why are you creating this piece of content?
- ☐ Bold Tagline
- ☐ Personal connection/story
- ☐ Call to Think or Call to Act
- ☐ Image (eye-catching and matches the story)

MONDAY	TUESDAY	WEDNESDAY
f FACEBOOK	**f**	**f**
⬤ INSTAGRAM	⬤	⬤
⊕ IG STORIES	⊕	⊕

THURSDAY	FRIDAY	SATURDAY	SUNDAY
f	f	f	f
ⓘ	ⓘ	ⓘ	ⓘ
⊕	⊕	⊕	⊕

REFLECT & REFINE

f

POST REACH ∧∨ _____

CURRENT # OF FOLLOWERS ∧∨ _____

MOST ENGAGING POST _____

_____

_____

SHARED / ORIGINAL (CIRCLE ONE)

⊙

ACCOUNTS REACHED ∧∨ _____

NEW FOLLOWERS _____

CURRENT FOLLOWERS _____

HIGHEST POST REACH:

_____

MOST SAVED CONTENT _____

MOST SHARED CONTENT _____

OF COLLABORATIONS _____

MOST STORY VIEWS _____

BUSINESS RESULTS

OF INVITES SENT? _____

OF CUSTOMERS ENROLLED? _____

INCOME I EARNED? _____

WEEK ENDING

👍 WIN > 🌀 PLOT TWIST

♡ WHY (SELF EVALUATION)

◎ BIZ GOALS FOR THE WEEK

\# 4 HASH METHOD

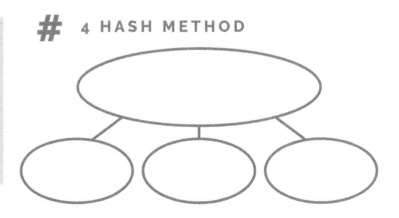

MY INCOME PRODUCING
ACTIVITY TRACKER

WEEK OF

		Mon	Tues	Weds	Thur	Fri	Sat	Sun
INCOME PRODUCING ACTIVITIES	**COMMUNITY**	Add Followers							
		Intentional Connect with Followers *not an invite							
		Social Media Post (4 Hash Method)							
		7-10 Stories							
		Highlight People: Testimonials/ Shout Outs							
	CONVERSION	DM people who viewed, liked, commented, or followed							
		Direct invite to service, experience, or product							
		Follow Ups							
	CUSTOMER SERVICE	Ask for Referrals							
		Engage with Current Clients							
		Answer Emails & Messages							
		Business Development							
		Personal Development							

WEEKLY SOCIAL MEDIA PLAN

THINGS TO CONSIDER

- Captions/Taglines
- Content I Like
- Hashtags
- Objections
- Collaborations
- Pain Points
- Well Received Content to Refurbish
- CTA's
- CTT's
- Quotables
- Community Driven Content
- Upcoming Events

CONTENT CREATION CHECKLIST

- [ ] Why are you creating this piece of content?
- [ ] Bold Tagline
- [ ] Personal connection/story
- [ ] Call to Think or Call to Act
- [ ] Image (eye-catching and matches the story)

MONDAY	TUESDAY	WEDNESDAY
f FACEBOOK	f	f
◎ INSTAGRAM	◎	◎
⊕ IG STORIES	⊕	⊕

THURSDAY	FRIDAY	SATURDAY	SUNDAY
f	f	f	f
⃝	⃝	⃝	⃝
⊕	⊕	⊕	⊕

month:

_____

marketing focus:

_____
_____
_____
_____
_____
_____
_____
_____
_____
_____

MONDAY	TUESDAY	WEDNESDAY

MONTHLY GOALS:

THURSDAY	FRIDAY	SATURDAY	SUNDAY

REFLECT & REFINE

f

POST REACH ︿⌄ _____

CURRENT # OF FOLLOWERS ︿⌄ _____

MOST ENGAGING POST _____

_____

_____

SHARED / ORIGINAL (CIRCLE ONE)

👍 WIN > 🌪 PLOT TWIST

♡ WHY (SELF EVALUATION)

◉

ACCOUNTS REACHED ︿⌄ _____

NEW FOLLOWERS _____

CURRENT FOLLOWERS _____

HIGHEST POST REACH:

_____

MOST SAVED CONTENT _____

MOST SHARED CONTENT _____

OF COLLABORATIONS _____

MOST STORY VIEWS _____

🎯 BIZ GOALS FOR THE WEEK

BUSINESS RESULTS

OF INVITES SENT? _____

OF CUSTOMERS ENROLLED? _____

INCOME I EARNED? _____

\# 4 HASH METHOD

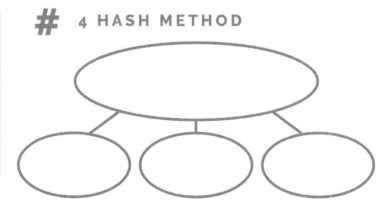

MY INCOME PRODUCING
ACTIVITY TRACKER

WEEK OF _____

		Mon	Tues	Weds	Thur	Fri	Sat	Sun
INCOME PRODUCING ACTIVITIES	**COMMUNITY**	Add Followers						
		Intentional Connect with Followers *not an invite						
		Social Media Post (4 Hash Method)						
		7-10 Stories						
		Highlight People: Testimonials/ Shout Outs						
	CONVERSION	DM people who viewed, liked, commented, or followed						
		Direct invite to service, experience, or product						
		Follow Ups						
	CUSTOMER SERVICE	Ask for Referrals						
		Engage with Current Clients						
		Answer Emails & Messages						
		Business Development						
		Personal Development						

WEEKLY SOCIAL MEDIA PLAN

THINGS TO CONSIDER

- Captions/Taglines
- Content I Like
- Hashtags
- Objections
- Collaborations
- Pain Points
- Well Received Content to Refurbish
- CTA's
- CTT's
- Quotables
- Community Driven Content
- Upcoming Events

CONTENT CREATION CHECKLIST

- ☐ Why are you creating this piece of content?
- ☐ Bold Tagline
- ☐ Personal connection/story
- ☐ Call to Think or Call to Act
- ☐ Image (eye-catching and matches the story)

MONDAY	TUESDAY	WEDNESDAY
f FACEBOOK	f	f
⃝ INSTAGRAM	⃝	⃝
⊕ IG STORIES	⊕	⊕

MY GOAL THIS WEEK:

THURSDAY	FRIDAY	SATURDAY	SUNDAY
f	f	f	f
ⓘ	ⓘ	ⓘ	ⓘ
⊕	⊕	⊕	⊕

REFLECT & REFINE

f

POST REACH ^v _____

CURRENT # OF FOLLOWERS ^v _____

MOST ENGAGING POST _____

_____

_____

SHARED / ORIGINAL (CIRCLE ONE)

⊙ (Instagram)

ACCOUNTS REACHED ^v _____

NEW FOLLOWERS _____

CURRENT FOLLOWERS _____

HIGHEST POST REACH:

_____

MOST SAVED CONTENT _____

MOST SHARED CONTENT _____

OF COLLABORATIONS _____

MOST STORY VIEWS _____

BUSINESS RESULTS

OF INVITES SENT? _____

OF CUSTOMERS ENROLLED? _____

INCOME I EARNED? _____

WEEK ENDING

_____

👍 **WIN** > 🌪 **PLOT TWIST**

♡ **WHY (SELF EVALUATION)**

◎ **BIZ GOALS FOR THE WEEK**

4 HASH METHOD

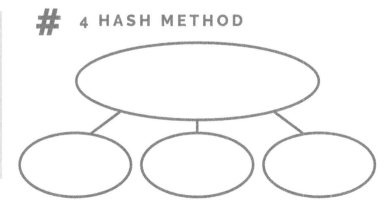

MY INCOME PRODUCING
ACTIVITY TRACKER

		Mon	Tues	Weds	Thur	Fri	Sat	Sun
INCOME PRODUCING ACTIVITIES	**COMMUNITY**	Add Followers						
		Intentional Connect with Followers *not an invite						
		Social Media Post (4 Hash Method)						
		7-10 Stories						
		Highlight People: Testimonials/ Shout Outs						
	CONVERSION	DM people who viewed, liked, commented, or followed						
		Direct invite to service, experience, or product						
		Follow Ups						
	CUSTOMER SERVICE	Ask for Referrals						
		Engage with Current Clients						
		Answer Emails & Messages						
		Business Development						
		Personal Development						

WEEKLY SOCIAL MEDIA PLAN

	MONDAY	TUESDAY	WEDNESDAY
	f FACEBOOK	f	f
	⃝ INSTAGRAM	⃝	⃝
	⊕ IG STORIES	⊕	⊕

THINGS TO CONSIDER

- Captions/Taglines
- Content I Like
- Hashtags
- Objections
- Collaborations
- Pain Points
- Well Received Content to Refurbish
- CTA's
- CTT's
- Quotables
- Community Driven Content
- Upcoming Events

CONTENT CREATION CHECKLIST

- ☐ Why are you creating this piece of content?
- ☐ Bold Tagline
- ☐ Personal connection/story
- ☐ Call to Think or Call to Act
- ☐ Image (eye-catching and matches the story)

MY GOAL THIS WEEK:

THURSDAY	FRIDAY	SATURDAY	SUNDAY
f	f	f	f
ⓘ	ⓘ	ⓘ	ⓘ
⊕	⊕	⊕	⊕

REFLECT & REFINE

f

POST REACH ∧∨ _____

CURRENT # OF FOLLOWERS ∧∨ _____

MOST ENGAGING POST _____

_____

_____

SHARED / ORIGINAL (CIRCLE ONE)

⊙ (Instagram)

ACCOUNTS REACHED ∧∨ _____

NEW FOLLOWERS _____

CURRENT FOLLOWERS _____

HIGHEST POST REACH:

_____

MOST SAVED CONTENT _____

MOST SHARED CONTENT _____

OF COLLABORATIONS _____

MOST STORY VIEWS _____

BUSINESS RESULTS

OF INVITES SENT? _____

OF CUSTOMERS ENROLLED? _____

INCOME I EARNED? _____

WEEK ENDING

👍 WIN > 🌪 PLOT TWIST

♡ WHY (SELF EVALUATION)

◎ BIZ GOALS FOR THE WEEK

4 HASH METHOD

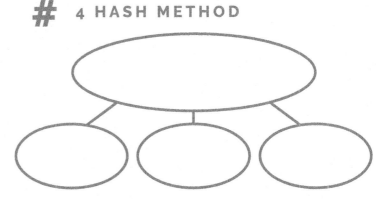

MY INCOME PRODUCING ACTIVITY TRACKER

			Mon	Tues	Weds	Thur	Fri	Sat	Sun
INCOME PRODUCING ACTIVITIES	**COMMUNITY**	Add Followers							
		Intentional Connect with Followers *not an invite							
		Social Media Post (4 Hash Method)							
		7-10 Stories							
		Highlight People: Testimonials/ Shout Outs							
	CONVERSION	DM people who viewed, liked, commented, or followed							
		Direct invite to service, experience, or product							
		Follow Ups							
	CUSTOMER SERVICE	Ask for Referrals							
		Engage with Current Clients							
		Answer Emails & Messages							
		Business Development							
		Personal Development							

WEEKLY SOCIAL MEDIA PLAN

THINGS TO CONSIDER

- Captions/Taglines
- Content I Like
- Hashtags
- Objections
- Collaborations
- Pain Points
- Well Received Content to Refurbish
- CTA's
- CTT's
- Quotables
- Community Driven Content
- Upcoming Events

CONTENT CREATION CHECKLIST

- ☐ Why are you creating this piece of content?
- ☐ Bold Tagline
- ☐ Personal connection/story
- ☐ Call to Think or Call to Act
- ☐ Image (eye-catching and matches the story)

MONDAY	TUESDAY	WEDNESDAY
f FACEBOOK	**f**	**f**
⃝ INSTAGRAM	⃝	⃝
⊕ IG STORIES	⊕	⊕

MY GOAL THIS WEEK:

THURSDAY	FRIDAY	SATURDAY	SUNDAY
f	f	f	f
⊙	⊙	⊙	⊙
⊕	⊕	⊕	⊕

REFLECT & REFINE

f

POST REACH ∧∨ _____

CURRENT # OF FOLLOWERS ∧∨ _____

MOST ENGAGING POST _____

_____

_____

SHARED / ORIGINAL (CIRCLE ONE)

ACCOUNTS REACHED ∧∨ _____

NEW FOLLOWERS _____

CURRENT FOLLOWERS _____

HIGHEST POST REACH:

_____

MOST SAVED CONTENT _____

MOST SHARED CONTENT _____

OF COLLABORATIONS _____

MOST STORY VIEWS _____

BUSINESS RESULTS

OF INVITES SENT? _____

OF CUSTOMERS ENROLLED? _____

INCOME I EARNED? _____

👍 WIN > 🌪 PLOT TWIST

♡ WHY (SELF EVALUATION)

🎯 BIZ GOALS FOR THE WEEK

4 HASH METHOD

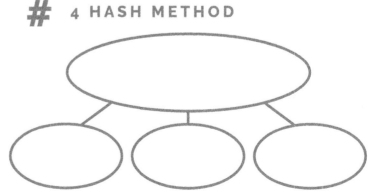

MY INCOME PRODUCING
ACTIVITY TRACKER

			Mon	Tues	Weds	Thur	Fri	Sat	Sun
INCOME PRODUCING ACTIVITIES	**COMMUNITY**	Add Followers							
		Intentional Connect with Followers *not an invite							
		Social Media Post (4 Hash Method)							
		7-10 Stories							
		Highlight People: Testimonials/ Shout Outs							
	CONVERSION	DM people who viewed, liked, commented, or followed							
		Direct invite to service, experience, or product							
		Follow Ups							
	CUSTOMER SERVICE	Ask for Referrals							
		Engage with Current Clients							
		Answer Emails & Messages							
		Business Development							
		Personal Development							

WEEKLY SOCIAL MEDIA PLAN

THINGS TO CONSIDER

- Captions/Taglines
- Content I Like
- Hashtags
- Objections
- Collaborations
- Pain Points
- Well Received Content to Refurbish
- CTA's
- CTT's
- Quotables
- Community Driven Content
- Upcoming Events

CONTENT CREATION CHECKLIST

- ☐ Why are you creating this piece of content?
- ☐ Bold Tagline
- ☐ Personal connection/story
- ☐ Call to Think or Call to Act
- ☐ Image (eye-catching and matches the story)

MONDAY	TUESDAY	WEDNESDAY
f FACEBOOK	**f**	**f**
⬡ INSTAGRAM	⬡	⬡
⊕ IG STORIES	⊕	⊕

THURSDAY	FRIDAY	SATURDAY	SUNDAY
f	f	f	f
(Instagram)	(Instagram)	(Instagram)	(Instagram)
(+)	(+)	(+)	(+)

REFLECT & REFINE

f _____

POST REACH ∧∨ _____

CURRENT # OF FOLLOWERS ∧∨ _____

MOST ENGAGING POST _____

_____

_____

SHARED / ORIGINAL (CIRCLE ONE)

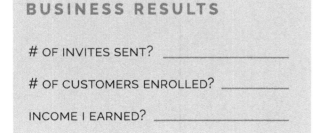

ACCOUNTS REACHED ∧∨ _____

NEW FOLLOWERS _____

CURRENT FOLLOWERS _____

HIGHEST POST REACH:

_____

MOST SAVED CONTENT _____

MOST SHARED CONTENT _____

OF COLLABORATIONS _____

MOST STORY VIEWS _____

BUSINESS RESULTS

OF INVITES SENT? _____

OF CUSTOMERS ENROLLED? _____

INCOME I EARNED? _____

👍 WIN > 🌪 PLOT TWIST

♡ WHY (SELF EVALUATION)

🎯 BIZ GOALS FOR THE WEEK

4 HASH METHOD

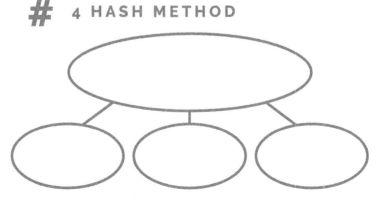

MY INCOME PRODUCING
ACTIVITY TRACKER

			Mon	Tues	Weds	Thur	Fri	Sat	Sun
INCOME PRODUCING ACTIVITIES	**COMMUNITY**	Add Followers							
		Intentional Connect with Followers *not an invite							
		Social Media Post (4 Hash Method)							
		7-10 Stories							
		Highlight People: Testimonials/ Shout Outs							
	CONVERSION	DM people who viewed, liked, commented, or followed							
		Direct invite to service, experience, or product							
		Follow Ups							
	CUSTOMER SERVICE	Ask for Referrals							
		Engage with Current Clients							
		Answer Emails & Messages							
		Business Development							
		Personal Development							

WEEKLY SOCIAL MEDIA PLAN

THINGS TO CONSIDER

- Captions/Taglines
- Content I Like
- Hashtags
- Objections
- Collaborations
- Pain Points
- Well Received
  Content to Refurbish
- CTA's
- CTT's
- Quotables
- Community Driven
  Content
- Upcoming Events

CONTENT CREATION CHECKLIST

- ☐ Why are you creating this piece of content?
- ☐ Bold Tagline
- ☐ Personal connection/story
- ☐ Call to Think or Call to Act
- ☐ Image (eye-catching and matches the story)

MONDAY	TUESDAY	WEDNESDAY
f FACEBOOK	**f**	**f**
⬡ INSTAGRAM	⬡	⬡
⊕ IG STORIES	⊕	⊕

THURSDAY	FRIDAY	SATURDAY	SUNDAY
f	f	f	f
⊡	⊡	⊡	⊡
⊕	⊕	⊕	⊕

month:

_____

*marketing
focus:*

_____

_____

_____

_____

_____

_____

_____

_____

_____

_____

_____

MONDAY	TUESDAY	WEDNESDAY

MONTHLY GOALS:

THURSDAY	FRIDAY	SATURDAY	SUNDAY

REFLECT & REFINE

f _____

POST REACH ∧∨ _____

CURRENT # OF FOLLOWERS ∧∨ _____

MOST ENGAGING POST _____

_____

_____

SHARED / ORIGINAL (CIRCLE ONE)

⃝ _____

ACCOUNTS REACHED ∧∨ _____

NEW FOLLOWERS _____

CURRENT FOLLOWERS _____

HIGHEST POST REACH:

_____

MOST SAVED CONTENT _____

MOST SHARED CONTENT _____

OF COLLABORATIONS _____

MOST STORY VIEWS _____

BUSINESS RESULTS

OF INVITES SENT? _____

OF CUSTOMERS ENROLLED? _____

INCOME I EARNED? _____

_____

WEEK ENDING

👍 WIN > 🌀 PLOT TWIST

♡ WHY (SELF EVALUATION)

🎯 BIZ GOALS FOR THE WEEK

4 HASH METHOD

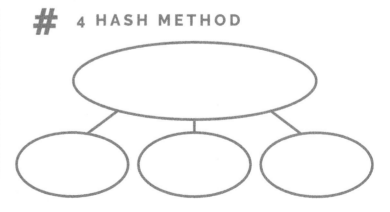

MY INCOME PRODUCING ACTIVITY TRACKER

		Mon	Tues	Weds	Thur	Fri	Sat	Sun
INCOME PRODUCING ACTIVITIES	**COMMUNITY**	Add Followers						
		Intentional Connect with Followers *not an invite						
		Social Media Post (4 Hash Method)						
		7-10 Stories						
		Highlight People: Testimonials/ Shout Outs						
	CONVERSION	DM people who viewed, liked, commented, or followed						
		Direct invite to service, experience, or product						
		Follow Ups						
	CUSTOMER SERVICE	Ask for Referrals						
		Engage with Current Clients						
		Answer Emails & Messages						
		Business Development						
		Personal Development						

WEEKLY SOCIAL MEDIA PLAN

THINGS TO CONSIDER

- Captions/Taglines
- Content I Like
- Hashtags
- Objections
- Collaborations
- Pain Points
- Well Received Content to Refurbish
- CTA's
- CTT's
- Quotables
- Community Driven Content
- Upcoming Events

CONTENT CREATION CHECKLIST

- ☐ Why are you creating this piece of content?
- ☐ Bold Tagline
- ☐ Personal connection/story
- ☐ Call to Think or Call to Act
- ☐ Image (eye-catching and matches the story)

MONDAY	TUESDAY	WEDNESDAY
f FACEBOOK	**f**	**f**
⃝ INSTAGRAM	⃝	⃝
⊕ IG STORIES	⊕	⊕

MY GOAL THIS WEEK:

THURSDAY	FRIDAY	SATURDAY	SUNDAY
f	f	f	f
ⓘ	ⓘ	ⓘ	ⓘ
⊕	⊕	⊕	⊕

REFLECT & REFINE

f

POST REACH ^∨ _____

CURRENT # OF FOLLOWERS ^∨ _____

MOST ENGAGING POST _____

_____

_____

SHARED / ORIGINAL (CIRCLE ONE)

ACCOUNTS REACHED ^∨ _____

NEW FOLLOWERS _____

CURRENT FOLLOWERS _____

HIGHEST POST REACH:

_____

MOST SAVED CONTENT _____

MOST SHARED CONTENT _____

OF COLLABORATIONS _____

MOST STORY VIEWS _____

BUSINESS RESULTS

OF INVITES SENT? _____

OF CUSTOMERS ENROLLED? _____

INCOME I EARNED? _____

WEEK ENDING

👍 WIN > 🌪 PLOT TWIST

♡ WHY (SELF EVALUATION)

🎯 BIZ GOALS FOR THE WEEK

4 HASH METHOD

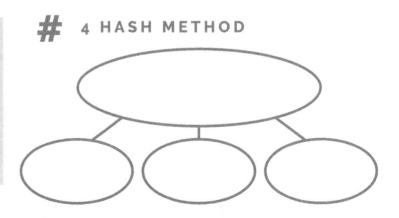

MY INCOME PRODUCING
ACTIVITY TRACKER

		Mon	Tues	Weds	Thur	Fri	Sat	Sun
INCOME PRODUCING ACTIVITIES	**COMMUNITY**	Add Followers						
		Intentional Connect with Followers *not an invite						
		Social Media Post (4 Hash Method)						
		7-10 Stories						
		Highlight People: Testimonials/ Shout Outs						
	CONVERSION	DM people who viewed, liked, com-mented, or followed						
		Direct invite to service, experience, or product						
		Follow Ups						
	CUSTOMER SERVICE	Ask for Referrals						
		Engage with Current Clients						
		Answer Emails & Messages						
		Business Development						
		Personal Development						

WEEKLY SOCIAL MEDIA PLAN

THINGS TO CONSIDER

- Captions/Taglines
- Content I Like
- Hashtags
- Objections
- Collaborations
- Pain Points
- Well Received Content to Refurbish
- CTA's
- CTT's
- Quotables
- Community Driven Content
- Upcoming Events

CONTENT CREATION CHECKLIST

- ☐ Why are you creating this piece of content?
- ☐ Bold Tagline
- ☐ Personal connection/story
- ☐ Call to Think or Call to Act
- ☐ Image (eye-catching and matches the story)

MONDAY	TUESDAY	WEDNESDAY
f FACEBOOK	**f**	**f**
◉ INSTAGRAM	◉	◉
⊕ IG STORIES	⊕	⊕

THURSDAY	FRIDAY	SATURDAY	SUNDAY
f	f	f	f
⊙	⊙	⊙	⊙
⊕	⊕	⊕	⊕

REFLECT & REFINE

f

POST REACH ^⌄ _____

CURRENT # OF FOLLOWERS ^⌄ _____

MOST ENGAGING POST _____

_____

_____

SHARED / ORIGINAL (CIRCLE ONE)

⊙

ACCOUNTS REACHED ^⌄ _____

NEW FOLLOWERS _____

CURRENT FOLLOWERS _____

HIGHEST POST REACH:

_____

MOST SAVED CONTENT _____

MOST SHARED CONTENT _____

OF COLLABORATIONS _____

MOST STORY VIEWS _____

BUSINESS RESULTS

OF INVITES SENT? _____

OF CUSTOMERS ENROLLED? _____

INCOME I EARNED? _____

_____

WEEK ENDING

👍 WIN > 🌪 PLOT TWIST

♡ WHY (SELF EVALUATION)

🎯 BIZ GOALS FOR THE WEEK

4 HASH METHOD

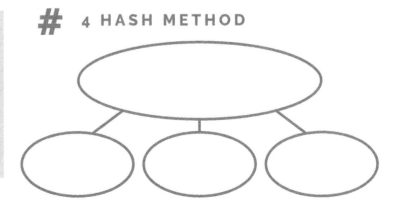

MY INCOME PRODUCING
ACTIVITY TRACKER

		Mon	Tues	Weds	Thur	Fri	Sat	Sun
INCOME PRODUCING ACTIVITIES	**COMMUNITY**	Add Followers						
		Intentional Connect with Followers *not an invite						
		Social Media Post (4 Hash Method)						
		7-10 Stories						
		Highlight People: Testimonials/ Shout Outs						
	CONVERSION	DM people who viewed, liked, commented, or followed						
		Direct invite to service, experience, or product						
		Follow Ups						
	CUSTOMER SERVICE	Ask for Referrals						
		Engage with Current Clients						
		Answer Emails & Messages						
		Business Development						
		Personal Development						

WEEKLY SOCIAL MEDIA PLAN

THINGS TO CONSIDER

- Captions/Taglines
- Content I Like
- Hashtags
- Objections
- Collaborations
- Pain Points
- Well Received Content to Refurbish
- CTA's
- CTT's
- Quotables
- Community Driven Content
- Upcoming Events

CONTENT CREATION CHECKLIST

- ☐ Why are you creating this piece of content?
- ☐ Bold Tagline
- ☐ Personal connection/story
- ☐ Call to Think or Call to Act
- ☐ Image (eye-catching and matches the story)

MONDAY	TUESDAY	WEDNESDAY
f FACEBOOK	f	f
ⓘ INSTAGRAM	ⓘ	ⓘ
⊕ IG STORIES	⊕	⊕

THURSDAY	FRIDAY	SATURDAY	SUNDAY
f	f	f	f
⌾	⌾	⌾	⌾
⊕	⊕	⊕	⊕

REFLECT & REFINE

f

POST REACH $\wedge$ _____

CURRENT # OF FOLLOWERS $\wedge$ _____

MOST ENGAGING POST _____

_____

_____

SHARED / ORIGINAL (CIRCLE ONE)

Instagram

ACCOUNTS REACHED $\wedge$ _____

NEW FOLLOWERS _____

CURRENT FOLLOWERS _____

HIGHEST POST REACH:

_____

MOST SAVED CONTENT _____

MOST SHARED CONTENT _____

OF COLLABORATIONS _____

MOST STORY VIEWS _____

BUSINESS RESULTS

OF INVITES SENT? _____

OF CUSTOMERS ENROLLED? _____

INCOME I EARNED? _____

WEEK ENDING

 WIN > PLOT TWIST

♡ WHY (SELF EVALUATION)

◎ BIZ GOALS FOR THE WEEK

4 HASH METHOD

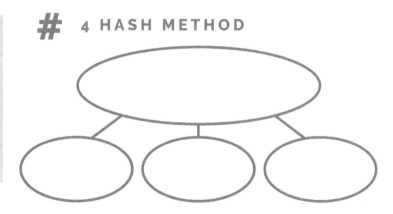

MY INCOME PRODUCING ACTIVITY TRACKER

WEEK OF

INCOME PRODUCING ACTIVITIES			Mon	Tues	Weds	Thur	Fri	Sat	Sun
	COMMUNITY	Add Followers							
		Intentional Connect with Followers *not an invite							
		Social Media Post (4 Hash Method)							
		7-10 Stories							
		Highlight People: Testimonials/ Shout Outs							
	CONVERSION	DM people who viewed, liked, commented, or followed							
		Direct invite to service, experience, or product							
		Follow Ups							
	CUSTOMER SERVICE	Ask for Referrals							
		Engage with Current Clients							
		Answer Emails & Messages							
		Business Development							
		Personal Development							

WEEKLY SOCIAL MEDIA PLAN

THINGS TO CONSIDER

- Captions/Taglines
- Content I Like
- Hashtags
- Objections
- Collaborations
- Pain Points
- Well Received Content to Refurbish
- CTA's
- CTT's
- Quotables
- Community Driven Content
- Upcoming Events

CONTENT CREATION CHECKLIST

- [ ] Why are you creating this piece of content?
- [ ] Bold Tagline
- [ ] Personal connection/story
- [ ] Call to Think or Call to Act
- [ ] Image (eye-catching and matches the story)

MONDAY	TUESDAY	WEDNESDAY
f FACEBOOK	**f**	**f**
(O) INSTAGRAM	(O)	(O)
(+) IG STORIES	(+)	(+)

THURSDAY	FRIDAY	SATURDAY	SUNDAY
f	f	f	f
⊙	⊙	⊙	⊙
⊕	⊕	⊕	⊕

REFLECT & REFINE

f

POST REACH ∧∨ _____

CURRENT # OF FOLLOWERS ∧∨ _____

MOST ENGAGING POST _____

_____

_____

SHARED / ORIGINAL (CIRCLE ONE)

📷

ACCOUNTS REACHED ∧∨ _____

NEW FOLLOWERS _____

CURRENT FOLLOWERS _____

HIGHEST POST REACH:

_____

MOST SAVED CONTENT _____

MOST SHARED CONTENT _____

OF COLLABORATIONS _____

MOST STORY VIEWS _____

BUSINESS RESULTS

OF INVITES SENT? _____

OF CUSTOMERS ENROLLED? _____

INCOME I EARNED? _____

👍 WIN > 🌪 PLOT TWIST

♡ WHY (SELF EVALUATION)

🎯 BIZ GOALS FOR THE WEEK

4 HASH METHOD

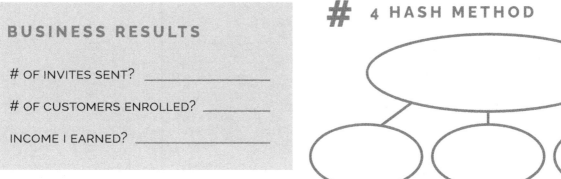

MY INCOME PRODUCING
ACTIVITY TRACKER

		Mon	Tues	Weds	Thur	Fri	Sat	Sun
INCOME PRODUCING ACTIVITIES	**COMMUNITY**	Add Followers							
		Intentional Connect with Followers *not an invite							
		Social Media Post (4 Hash Method)							
		7-10 Stories							
		Highlight People: Testimonials/ Shout Outs							
	CONVERSION	DM people who viewed, liked, commented, or followed							
		Direct invite to service, experience, or product							
		Follow Ups							
	CUSTOMER SERVICE	Ask for Referrals							
		Engage with Current Clients							
		Answer Emails & Messages							
		Business Development							
		Personal Development							

WEEKLY SOCIAL MEDIA PLAN

THINGS TO CONSIDER

- Captions/Taglines
- Content I Like
- Hashtags
- Objections
- Collaborations
- Pain Points
- Well Received Content to Refurbish
- CTA's
- CTT's
- Quotables
- Community Driven Content
- Upcoming Events

CONTENT CREATION CHECKLIST

- [ ] Why are you creating this piece of content?
- [ ] Bold Tagline
- [ ] Personal connection/story
- [ ] Call to Think or Call to Act
- [ ] Image (eye-catching and matches the story)

MONDAY	TUESDAY	WEDNESDAY
f FACEBOOK	f	f
🅾 INSTAGRAM	🅾	🅾
⊕ IG STORIES	⊕	⊕

THURSDAY	FRIDAY	SATURDAY	SUNDAY
f	f	f	f
ⓘ	ⓘ	ⓘ	ⓘ
⊕	⊕	⊕	⊕

month:

_____

marketing focus:

_____
_____
_____
_____
_____
_____
_____
_____
_____
_____

MONDAY	TUESDAY	WEDNESDAY

MONTHLY GOALS:

THURSDAY	FRIDAY	SATURDAY	SUNDAY

REFLECT & REFINE

f _____

POST REACH ˄˅ _____

CURRENT # OF FOLLOWERS ˄˅ _____

MOST ENGAGING POST _____

_____

_____

SHARED / ORIGINAL (CIRCLE ONE)

ACCOUNTS REACHED ˄˅ _____

NEW FOLLOWERS _____

CURRENT FOLLOWERS _____

HIGHEST POST REACH:

_____

MOST SAVED CONTENT _____

MOST SHARED CONTENT _____

OF COLLABORATIONS _____

MOST STORY VIEWS _____

BUSINESS RESULTS

OF INVITES SENT? _____

OF CUSTOMERS ENROLLED? _____

INCOME I EARNED? _____

WEEK ENDING

👍 WIN > 🌪 PLOT TWIST

♡ WHY (SELF EVALUATION)

🎯 BIZ GOALS FOR THE WEEK

4 HASH METHOD

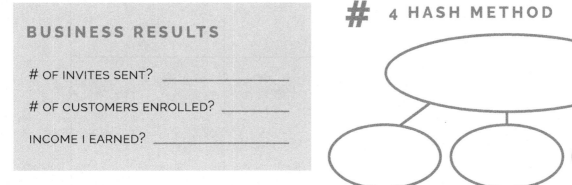

MY INCOME PRODUCING
ACTIVITY TRACKER

WEEK OF _____

			Mon	Tues	Weds	Thur	Fri	Sat	Sun
INCOME PRODUCING ACTIVITIES	**COMMUNITY**	Add Followers							
		Intentional Connect with Followers *not an invite							
		Social Media Post (4 Hash Method)							
		7-10 Stories							
		Highlight People: Testimonials/ Shout Outs							
	CONVERSION	DM people who viewed, liked, commented, or followed							
		Direct invite to service, experience, or product							
		Follow Ups							
	CUSTOMER SERVICE	Ask for Referrals							
		Engage with Current Clients							
		Answer Emails & Messages							
		Business Development							
		Personal Development							

WEEKLY SOCIAL MEDIA PLAN

THINGS TO CONSIDER

- Captions/Taglines
- Content I Like
- Hashtags
- Objections
- Collaborations
- Pain Points
- Well Received Content to Refurbish
- CTA's
- CTT's
- Quotables
- Community Driven Content
- Upcoming Events

CONTENT CREATION CHECKLIST

- ☐ Why are you creating this piece of content?
- ☐ Bold Tagline
- ☐ Personal connection/story
- ☐ Call to Think or Call to Act
- ☐ Image (eye-catching and matches the story)

MONDAY	TUESDAY	WEDNESDAY
f FACEBOOK	**f**	**f**
ⓞ INSTAGRAM	ⓞ	ⓞ
⊕ IG STORIES	⊕	⊕

THURSDAY	FRIDAY	SATURDAY	SUNDAY
f	f	f	f

REFLECT & REFINE

f _____

POST REACH ^∨ _____

CURRENT # OF FOLLOWERS ^∨ _____

MOST ENGAGING POST _____

_____

_____

SHARED / ORIGINAL (CIRCLE ONE)

⊙ _____

ACCOUNTS REACHED ^∨ _____

NEW FOLLOWERS _____

CURRENT FOLLOWERS _____

HIGHEST POST REACH:

_____

MOST SAVED CONTENT _____

MOST SHARED CONTENT _____

OF COLLABORATIONS _____

MOST STORY VIEWS _____

BUSINESS RESULTS

OF INVITES SENT? _____

OF CUSTOMERS ENROLLED? _____

INCOME I EARNED? _____

WEEK ENDING

👍 WIN > 🌪 PLOT TWIST

♡ WHY (SELF EVALUATION)

🎯 BIZ GOALS FOR THE WEEK

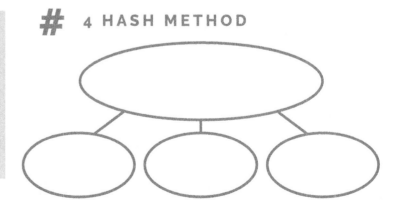

4 HASH METHOD

MY INCOME PRODUCING
ACTIVITY TRACKER

			Mon	Tues	Weds	Thur	Fri	Sat	Sun
INCOME PRODUCING ACTIVITIES	**COMMUNITY**	Add Followers							
		Intentional Connect with Followers *not an invite							
		Social Media Post (4 Hash Method)							
		7-10 Stories							
		Highlight People: Testimonials/ Shout Outs							
	CONVERSION	DM people who viewed, liked, commented, or followed							
		Direct invite to service, experience, or product							
		Follow Ups							
	CUSTOMER SERVICE	Ask for Referrals							
		Engage with Current Clients							
		Answer Emails & Messages							
		Business Development							
		Personal Development							

WEEKLY SOCIAL MEDIA PLAN

THINGS TO CONSIDER

- Captions/Taglines
- Content I Like
- Hashtags
- Objections
- Collaborations
- Pain Points
- Well Received Content to Refurbish
- CTA's
- CTT's
- Quotables
- Community Driven Content
- Upcoming Events

CONTENT CREATION CHECKLIST

- ☐ Why are you creating this piece of content?
- ☐ Bold Tagline
- ☐ Personal connection/story
- ☐ Call to Think or Call to Act
- ☐ Image (eye-catching and matches the story)

MONDAY	TUESDAY	WEDNESDAY
f FACEBOOK	f	f
⊙ INSTAGRAM	⊙	⊙
⊕ IG STORIES	⊕	⊕

MY GOAL THIS WEEK:

THURSDAY	FRIDAY	SATURDAY	SUNDAY
f	f	f	f
⬛	⬛	⬛	⬛
⊕	⊕	⊕	⊕

REFLECT & REFINE

f

POST REACH ^∨ _____

CURRENT # OF FOLLOWERS ^∨ _____

MOST ENGAGING POST _____

_____

_____

SHARED / ORIGINAL (CIRCLE ONE)

(Instagram)

ACCOUNTS REACHED ^∨ _____

NEW FOLLOWERS _____

CURRENT FOLLOWERS _____

HIGHEST POST REACH:

_____

MOST SAVED CONTENT _____

MOST SHARED CONTENT _____

OF COLLABORATIONS _____

MOST STORY VIEWS _____

BUSINESS RESULTS

OF INVITES SENT? _____

OF CUSTOMERS ENROLLED? _____

INCOME I EARNED? _____

WEEK ENDING

👍 WIN > 🌪 PLOT TWIST

♡ WHY (SELF EVALUATION)

🎯 BIZ GOALS FOR THE WEEK

4 HASH METHOD

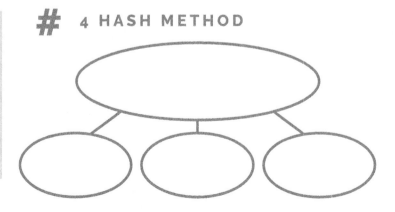

MY INCOME PRODUCING
ACTIVITY TRACKER

			Mon	Tues	Weds	Thur	Fri	Sat	Sun
INCOME PRODUCING ACTIVITIES	**COMMUNITY**	Add Followers							
		Intentional Connect with Followers *not an invite							
		Social Media Post (4 Hash Method)							
		7-10 Stories							
		Highlight People: Testimonials/ Shout Outs							
	CONVERSION	DM people who viewed, liked, commented, or followed							
		Direct invite to service, experience, or product							
		Follow Ups							
	CUSTOMER SERVICE	Ask for Referrals							
		Engage with Current Clients							
		Answer Emails & Messages							
		Business Development							
		Personal Development							

WEEKLY SOCIAL MEDIA PLAN

THINGS TO CONSIDER

- Captions/Taglines
- Content I Like
- Hashtags
- Objections
- Collaborations
- Pain Points
- Well Received Content to Refurbish
- CTA's
- CTT's
- Quotables
- Community Driven Content
- Upcoming Events

CONTENT CREATION CHECKLIST

- ☐ Why are you creating this piece of content?
- ☐ Bold Tagline
- ☐ Personal connection/story
- ☐ Call to Think or Call to Act
- ☐ Image (eye-catching and matches the story)

MONDAY	TUESDAY	WEDNESDAY
f FACEBOOK	f	f
⊙ INSTAGRAM	⊙	⊙
⊕ IG STORIES	⊕	⊕

THURSDAY	FRIDAY	SATURDAY	SUNDAY
f	f	f	f
⊙	⊙	⊙	⊙
⊕	⊕	⊕	⊕

REFLECT & REFINE

f

POST REACH ⌃⌄ _____

CURRENT # OF FOLLOWERS ⌃⌄ _____

MOST ENGAGING POST _____

_____

_____

SHARED / ORIGINAL (CIRCLE ONE)

Instagram

ACCOUNTS REACHED ⌃⌄ _____

NEW FOLLOWERS _____

CURRENT FOLLOWERS _____

HIGHEST POST REACH:

_____

MOST SAVED CONTENT _____

MOST SHARED CONTENT _____

OF COLLABORATIONS _____

MOST STORY VIEWS _____

BUSINESS RESULTS

OF INVITES SENT? _____

OF CUSTOMERS ENROLLED? _____

INCOME I EARNED? _____

WEEK ENDING

👍 WIN > 🌪 PLOT TWIST

♡ WHY (SELF EVALUATION)

◎ BIZ GOALS FOR THE WEEK

\# 4 HASH METHOD

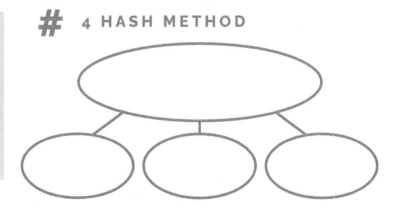

MY INCOME PRODUCING ACTIVITY TRACKER

WEEK OF _____

		Mon	Tues	Weds	Thur	Fri	Sat	Sun
INCOME PRODUCING ACTIVITIES	**COMMUNITY**	Add Followers							
		Intentional Connect with Followers *not an invite							
		Social Media Post (4 Hash Method)							
		7-10 Stories							
		Highlight People: Testimonials/ Shout Outs							
	CONVERSION	DM people who viewed, liked, commented, or followed							
		Direct invite to service, experience, or product							
		Follow Ups							
	CUSTOMER SERVICE	Ask for Referrals							
		Engage with Current Clients							
		Answer Emails & Messages							
		Business Development							
		Personal Development							

WEEKLY SOCIAL MEDIA PLAN

THINGS TO CONSIDER

- Captions/Taglines
- Content I Like
- Hashtags
- Objections
- Collaborations
- Pain Points
- Well Received Content to Refurbish
- CTA's
- CTT's
- Quotables
- Community Driven Content
- Upcoming Events

CONTENT CREATION CHECKLIST

- ☐ Why are you creating this piece of content?
- ☐ Bold Tagline
- ☐ Personal connection/story
- ☐ Call to Think or Call to Act
- ☐ Image (eye-catching and matches the story)

MONDAY	TUESDAY	WEDNESDAY
f FACEBOOK	**f**	**f**
◎ INSTAGRAM	◎	◎
⊕ IG STORIES	⊕	⊕

THURSDAY	FRIDAY	SATURDAY	SUNDAY
f	f	f	f
o	o	o	o
⊕	⊕	⊕	⊕

REFLECT & REFINE

f

POST REACH ⌃⌄ _____

CURRENT # OF FOLLOWERS ⌃⌄ _____

MOST ENGAGING POST _____

_____

_____

SHARED / ORIGINAL (CIRCLE ONE)

⊙

ACCOUNTS REACHED ⌃⌄ _____

NEW FOLLOWERS _____

CURRENT FOLLOWERS _____

HIGHEST POST REACH:

_____

MOST SAVED CONTENT _____

MOST SHARED CONTENT _____

OF COLLABORATIONS _____

MOST STORY VIEWS _____

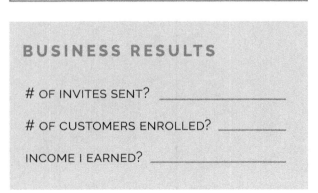

BUSINESS RESULTS

OF INVITES SENT? _____

OF CUSTOMERS ENROLLED? _____

INCOME I EARNED? _____

WEEK ENDING

👍 **WIN >** 🌪 **PLOT TWIST**

♡ **WHY (SELF EVALUATION)**

◎ **BIZ GOALS FOR THE WEEK**

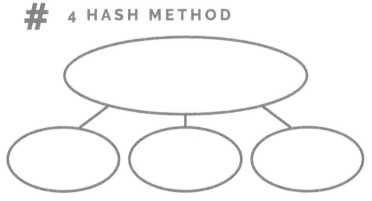

**4 HASH METHOD**

MY INCOME PRODUCING ACTIVITY TRACKER

			Mon	Tues	Weds	Thur	Fri	Sat	Sun
INCOME PRODUCING ACTIVITIES	**COMMUNITY**	Add Followers							
		Intentional Connect with Followers *not an invite							
		Social Media Post (4 Hash Method)							
		7-10 Stories							
		Highlight People: Testimonials/ Shout Outs							
	CONVERSION	DM people who viewed, liked, commented, or followed							
		Direct invite to service, experience, or product							
		Follow Ups							
	CUSTOMER SERVICE	Ask for Referrals							
		Engage with Current Clients							
		Answer Emails & Messages							
		Business Development							
		Personal Development							

WEEKLY SOCIAL MEDIA PLAN

THINGS TO CONSIDER

- Captions/Taglines
- Content I Like
- Hashtags
- Objections
- Collaborations
- Pain Points
- Well Received Content to Refurbish
- CTA's
- CTT's
- Quotables
- Community Driven Content
- Upcoming Events

CONTENT CREATION CHECKLIST

- ☐ Why are you creating this piece of content?
- ☐ Bold Tagline
- ☐ Personal connection/story
- ☐ Call to Think or Call to Act
- ☐ Image (eye-catching and matches the story)

MONDAY	TUESDAY	WEDNESDAY
f FACEBOOK	**f**	**f**
⃝ INSTAGRAM	⃝	⃝
⊕ IG STORIES	⊕	⊕

MY GOAL THIS WEEK:

THURSDAY	FRIDAY	SATURDAY	SUNDAY
f	f	f	f
⃝	⃝	⃝	⃝
⊕	⊕	⊕	⊕

month:

_____

marketing focus:

_____

_____

_____

_____

_____

_____

_____

_____

_____

_____

MONDAY	TUESDAY	WEDNESDAY

MONTHLY GOALS:

THURSDAY	FRIDAY	SATURDAY	SUNDAY

REFLECT & REFINE

f

POST REACH ∧∨ _____

CURRENT # OF FOLLOWERS ∧∨ _____

MOST ENGAGING POST _____

_____

_____

SHARED / ORIGINAL (CIRCLE ONE)

📷

ACCOUNTS REACHED ∧∨ _____

NEW FOLLOWERS _____

CURRENT FOLLOWERS _____

HIGHEST POST REACH:

_____

MOST SAVED CONTENT _____

MOST SHARED CONTENT _____

OF COLLABORATIONS _____

MOST STORY VIEWS _____

👍 WIN > 🌪 PLOT TWIST

♡ WHY (SELF EVALUATION)

🎯 BIZ GOALS FOR THE WEEK

BUSINESS RESULTS

OF INVITES SENT? _____

OF CUSTOMERS ENROLLED? _____

INCOME I EARNED? _____

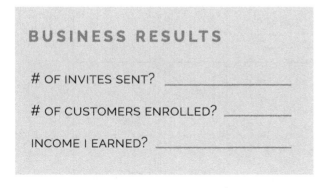

4 HASH METHOD

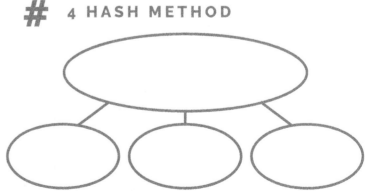

MY INCOME PRODUCING ACTIVITY TRACKER

WEEK OF

		Mon	Tues	Weds	Thur	Fri	Sat	Sun
INCOME PRODUCING ACTIVITIES	**COMMUNITY**	Add Followers						
		Intentional Connect with Followers *not an invite						
		Social Media Post (4 Hash Method)						
		7-10 Stories						
		Highlight People: Testimonials/ Shout Outs						
	CONVERSION	DM people who viewed, liked, commented, or followed						
		Direct invite to service, experience, or product						
		Follow Ups						
	CUSTOMER SERVICE	Ask for Referrals						
		Engage with Current Clients						
		Answer Emails & Messages						
		Business Development						
		Personal Development						

WEEKLY SOCIAL MEDIA PLAN

THINGS TO CONSIDER

- Captions/Taglines
- Content I Like
- Hashtags
- Objections
- Collaborations
- Pain Points
- Well Received Content to Refurbish
- CTA's
- CTT's
- Quotables
- Community Driven Content
- Upcoming Events

CONTENT CREATION CHECKLIST

- ☐ Why are you creating this piece of content?
- ☐ Bold Tagline
- ☐ Personal connection/story
- ☐ Call to Think or Call to Act
- ☐ Image (eye-catching and matches the story)

MONDAY	TUESDAY	WEDNESDAY
f FACEBOOK	**f**	**f**
⃝ INSTAGRAM	⃝	⃝
⊕ IG STORIES	⊕	⊕

MY GOAL THIS WEEK:

THURSDAY	FRIDAY	SATURDAY	SUNDAY
f	f	f	f
ⓞ	ⓞ	ⓞ	ⓞ
⊕	⊕	⊕	⊕

REFLECT & REFINE

f

POST REACH ∧∨ _____

CURRENT # OF FOLLOWERS ∧∨ _____

MOST ENGAGING POST _____

_____

_____

SHARED / ORIGINAL (CIRCLE ONE)

◉

ACCOUNTS REACHED ∧∨ _____

NEW FOLLOWERS _____

CURRENT FOLLOWERS _____

HIGHEST POST REACH:

_____

MOST SAVED CONTENT _____

MOST SHARED CONTENT _____

OF COLLABORATIONS _____

MOST STORY VIEWS _____

BUSINESS RESULTS

OF INVITES SENT? _____

OF CUSTOMERS ENROLLED? _____

INCOME I EARNED? _____

WEEK ENDING

👍 WIN > 🌪 PLOT TWIST

♡ WHY (SELF EVALUATION)

◎ BIZ GOALS FOR THE WEEK

4 HASH METHOD

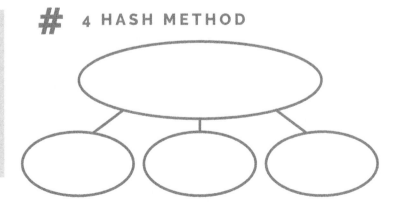

MY INCOME PRODUCING
ACTIVITY TRACKER

		Mon	Tues	Weds	Thur	Fri	Sat	Sun
INCOME PRODUCING ACTIVITIES	**COMMUNITY**	Add Followers						
		Intentional Connect with Followers *not an invite						
		Social Media Post (4 Hash Method)						
		7-10 Stories						
		Highlight People: Testimonials/ Shout Outs						
	CONVERSION	DM people who viewed, liked, commented, or followed						
		Direct invite to service, experience, or product						
		Follow Ups						
	CUSTOMER SERVICE	Ask for Referrals						
		Engage with Current Clients						
		Answer Emails & Messages						
		Business Development						
		Personal Development						

WEEKLY SOCIAL MEDIA PLAN

THINGS TO CONSIDER

- Captions/Taglines
- Content I Like
- Hashtags
- Objections
- Collaborations
- Pain Points
- Well Received Content to Refurbish
- CTA's
- CTT's
- Quotables
- Community Driven Content
- Upcoming Events

CONTENT CREATION CHECKLIST

- ☐ Why are you creating this piece of content?
- ☐ Bold Tagline
- ☐ Personal connection/story
- ☐ Call to Think or Call to Act
- ☐ Image (eye-catching and matches the story)

MONDAY	TUESDAY	WEDNESDAY
f FACEBOOK	f	f
⃝ INSTAGRAM	⃝	⃝
⊕ IG STORIES	⊕	⊕

MY GOAL THIS WEEK:

THURSDAY	FRIDAY	SATURDAY	SUNDAY
f	f	f	f
⊙	⊙	⊙	⊙
⊕	⊕	⊕	⊕

REFLECT & REFINE

f

POST REACH ^v _____

CURRENT # OF FOLLOWERS ^v _____

MOST ENGAGING POST _____

_____

_____

SHARED / ORIGINAL (CIRCLE ONE)

ACCOUNTS REACHED ^v _____

NEW FOLLOWERS _____

CURRENT FOLLOWERS _____

HIGHEST POST REACH:

_____

MOST SAVED CONTENT _____

MOST SHARED CONTENT _____

OF COLLABORATIONS _____

MOST STORY VIEWS _____

BUSINESS RESULTS

OF INVITES SENT? _____

OF CUSTOMERS ENROLLED? _____

INCOME I EARNED? _____

WEEK ENDING

👍 **WIN >** 🌪 **PLOT TWIST**

♡ **WHY (SELF EVALUATION)**

🎯 **BIZ GOALS FOR THE WEEK**

**4 HASH METHOD**

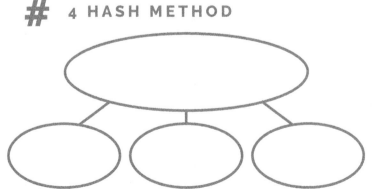

MY INCOME PRODUCING ACTIVITY TRACKER

		Mon	Tues	Weds	Thur	Fri	Sat	Sun
INCOME PRODUCING ACTIVITIES	**COMMUNITY**	**Add Followers**						
		Intentional Connect with Followers *not an invite						
		Social Media Post (4 Hash Method)						
		7-10 Stories						
		Highlight People: Testimonials/ Shout Outs						
	CONVERSION	**DM people who viewed, liked, commented, or followed**						
		Direct invite to service, experience, or product						
		Follow Ups						
	CUSTOMER SERVICE	**Ask for Referrals**						
		Engage with Current Clients						
		Answer Emails & Messages						
		Business Development						
		Personal Development						

WEEKLY SOCIAL MEDIA PLAN

THINGS TO CONSIDER

- Captions/Taglines
- Content I Like
- Hashtags
- Objections
- Collaborations
- Pain Points
- Well Received Content to Refurbish
- CTA's
- CTT's
- Quotables
- Community Driven Content
- Upcoming Events

CONTENT CREATION CHECKLIST

- ☐ Why are you creating this piece of content?
- ☐ Bold Tagline
- ☐ Personal connection/story
- ☐ Call to Think or Call to Act
- ☐ Image (eye-catching and matches the story)

MONDAY	TUESDAY	WEDNESDAY
f FACEBOOK	**f**	**f**
INSTAGRAM		
(+) IG STORIES	(+)	(+)

THURSDAY	FRIDAY	SATURDAY	SUNDAY
f	f	f	f
◉	◉	◉	◉
⊕	⊕	⊕	⊕

REFLECT & REFINE

f

POST REACH ∧∨ _____

CURRENT # OF FOLLOWERS ∧∨ _____

MOST ENGAGING POST _____

_____

_____

SHARED / ORIGINAL (CIRCLE ONE)

📷

ACCOUNTS REACHED ∧∨ _____

NEW FOLLOWERS _____

CURRENT FOLLOWERS _____

HIGHEST POST REACH:

_____

MOST SAVED CONTENT _____

MOST SHARED CONTENT _____

OF COLLABORATIONS _____

MOST STORY VIEWS _____

BUSINESS RESULTS

OF INVITES SENT? _____

OF CUSTOMERS ENROLLED? _____

INCOME I EARNED? _____

WEEK ENDING

👍 WIN > 🌪 PLOT TWIST

♡ WHY (SELF EVALUATION)

🎯 BIZ GOALS FOR THE WEEK

\# 4 HASH METHOD

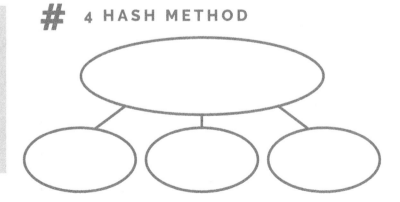

MY INCOME PRODUCING ACTIVITY TRACKER

WEEK OF _____

		Mon	Tues	Weds	Thur	Fri	Sat	Sun
INCOME PRODUCING ACTIVITIES	**COMMUNITY**	Add Followers						
		Intentional Connect with Followers *not an invite						
		Social Media Post (4 Hash Method)						
		7-10 Stories						
		Highlight People: Testimonials/ Shout Outs						
	CONVERSION	DM people who viewed, liked, commented, or followed						
		Direct invite to service, experience, or product						
		Follow Ups						
	CUSTOMER SERVICE	Ask for Referrals						
		Engage with Current Clients						
		Answer Emails & Messages						
		Business Development						
		Personal Development						

WEEKLY SOCIAL MEDIA PLAN

THINGS TO CONSIDER

- Captions/Taglines
- Content I Like
- Hashtags
- Objections
- Collaborations
- Pain Points
- Well Received Content to Refurbish
- CTA's
- CTT's
- Quotables
- Community Driven Content
- Upcoming Events

CONTENT CREATION CHECKLIST

- ☐ Why are you creating this piece of content?
- ☐ Bold Tagline
- ☐ Personal connection/story
- ☐ Call to Think or Call to Act
- ☐ Image (eye-catching and matches the story)

MONDAY	TUESDAY	WEDNESDAY
f FACEBOOK	f	f
◉ INSTAGRAM	◉	◉
⊕ IG STORIES	⊕	⊕

THURSDAY	FRIDAY	SATURDAY	SUNDAY
f	f	f	f
🅞	🅞	🅞	🅞
⊕	⊕	⊕	⊕

REFLECT & REFINE

f

POST REACH $\wedge$ $\vee$ _____

CURRENT # OF FOLLOWERS $\wedge$ $\vee$ _____

MOST ENGAGING POST _____

_____

_____

SHARED / ORIGINAL (CIRCLE ONE)

Instagram

ACCOUNTS REACHED $\wedge$ $\vee$ _____

NEW FOLLOWERS _____

CURRENT FOLLOWERS _____

HIGHEST POST REACH:

_____

MOST SAVED CONTENT _____

MOST SHARED CONTENT _____

OF COLLABORATIONS _____

MOST STORY VIEWS _____

BUSINESS RESULTS

OF INVITES SENT? _____

OF CUSTOMERS ENROLLED? _____

INCOME I EARNED? _____

WEEK ENDING

👍 WIN > 🌪 PLOT TWIST

♡ WHY (SELF EVALUATION)

◎ BIZ GOALS FOR THE WEEK

4 HASH METHOD

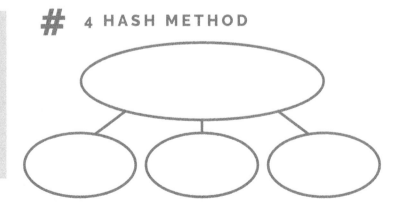

MY INCOME PRODUCING
ACTIVITY TRACKER

		Mon	Tues	Weds	Thur	Fri	Sat	Sun
INCOME PRODUCING ACTIVITIES	**COMMUNITY**	Add Followers						
		Intentional Connect with Followers *not an invite						
		Social Media Post (4 Hash Method)						
		7-10 Stories						
		Highlight People: Testimonials/ Shout Outs						
	CONVERSION	DM people who viewed, liked, commented, or followed						
		Direct invite to service, experience, or product						
		Follow Ups						
	CUSTOMER SERVICE	Ask for Referrals						
		Engage with Current Clients						
		Answer Emails & Messages						
		Business Development						
		Personal Development						

WEEKLY SOCIAL MEDIA PLAN

THINGS TO CONSIDER

- Captions/Taglines
- Content I Like
- Hashtags
- Objections
- Collaborations
- Pain Points
- Well Received Content to Refurbish
- CTA's
- CTT's
- Quotables
- Community Driven Content
- Upcoming Events

CONTENT CREATION CHECKLIST

- ☐ Why are you creating this piece of content?
- ☐ Bold Tagline
- ☐ Personal connection/story
- ☐ Call to Think or Call to Act
- ☐ Image (eye-catching and matches the story)

MONDAY	TUESDAY	WEDNESDAY
f FACEBOOK	**f**	**f**
⦿ INSTAGRAM	⦿	⦿
⊕ IG STORIES	⊕	⊕

THURSDAY	FRIDAY	SATURDAY	SUNDAY
f	f	f	f
⊙	⊙	⊙	⊙
⊕	⊕	⊕	⊕

month:

_____

*marketing
focus:*

_____
_____
_____
_____
_____
_____
_____
_____
_____
_____

MONDAY	TUESDAY	WEDNESDAY

MONTHLY GOALS:

THURSDAY	FRIDAY	SATURDAY	SUNDAY

REFLECT & REFINE

f

POST REACH ^∨ _____

CURRENT # OF FOLLOWERS ^∨ _____

MOST ENGAGING POST _____

_____

_____

SHARED / ORIGINAL (CIRCLE ONE)

📷

ACCOUNTS REACHED ^∨ _____

NEW FOLLOWERS _____

CURRENT FOLLOWERS _____

HIGHEST POST REACH:

_____

MOST SAVED CONTENT _____

MOST SHARED CONTENT _____

OF COLLABORATIONS _____

MOST STORY VIEWS _____

BUSINESS RESULTS

OF INVITES SENT? _____

OF CUSTOMERS ENROLLED? _____

INCOME I EARNED? _____

WEEK ENDING

👍 WIN > 🌪 PLOT TWIST

♡ WHY (SELF EVALUATION)

🎯 BIZ GOALS FOR THE WEEK

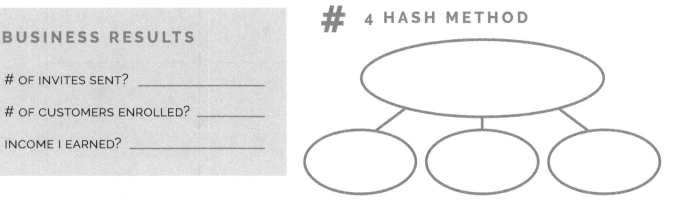

4 HASH METHOD

MY INCOME PRODUCING
ACTIVITY TRACKER

		Mon	Tues	Weds	Thur	Fri	Sat	Sun
INCOME PRODUCING ACTIVITIES	**COMMUNITY**	Add Followers						
		Intentional Connect with Followers *not an invite						
		Social Media Post (4 Hash Method)						
		7-10 Stories						
		Highlight People: Testimonials/ Shout Outs						
	CONVERSION	DM people who viewed, liked, commented, or followed						
		Direct invite to service, experience, or product						
		Follow Ups						
	CUSTOMER SERVICE	Ask for Referrals						
		Engage with Current Clients						
		Answer Emails & Messages						
		Business Development						
		Personal Development						

WEEKLY SOCIAL MEDIA PLAN

THINGS TO CONSIDER

- Captions/Taglines
- Content I Like
- Hashtags
- Objections
- Collaborations
- Pain Points
- Well Received Content to Refurbish
- CTA's
- CTT's
- Quotables
- Community Driven Content
- Upcoming Events

CONTENT CREATION CHECKLIST

- [ ] Why are you creating this piece of content?
- [ ] Bold Tagline
- [ ] Personal connection/story
- [ ] Call to Think or Call to Act
- [ ] Image (eye-catching and matches the story)

MONDAY	TUESDAY	WEDNESDAY
f FACEBOOK	**f**	**f**
⃝ INSTAGRAM	⃝	⃝
⊕ IG STORIES	⊕	⊕

MY GOAL THIS WEEK:

THURSDAY	FRIDAY	SATURDAY	SUNDAY
f	f	f	f
⃝	⃝	⃝	⃝
⊕	⊕	⊕	⊕

REFLECT & REFINE

f

POST REACH ^∨ _____

CURRENT # OF FOLLOWERS ^∨ _____

MOST ENGAGING POST _____

_____

_____

SHARED / ORIGINAL (CIRCLE ONE)

⊙ (Instagram)

ACCOUNTS REACHED ^∨ _____

NEW FOLLOWERS _____

CURRENT FOLLOWERS _____

HIGHEST POST REACH:

_____

MOST SAVED CONTENT _____

MOST SHARED CONTENT _____

OF COLLABORATIONS _____

MOST STORY VIEWS _____

BUSINESS RESULTS

OF INVITES SENT? _____

OF CUSTOMERS ENROLLED? _____

INCOME I EARNED? _____

WEEK ENDING

👍 WIN > 🌪 PLOT TWIST

♡ WHY (SELF EVALUATION)

🎯 BIZ GOALS FOR THE WEEK

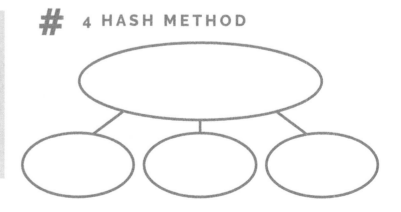

\# 4 HASH METHOD

MY INCOME PRODUCING ACTIVITY TRACKER

		Mon	Tues	Weds	Thur	Fri	Sat	Sun
INCOME PRODUCING ACTIVITIES	**COMMUNITY**	Add Followers						
		Intentional Connect with Followers *not an invite						
		Social Media Post (4 Hash Method)						
		7-10 Stories						
		Highlight People: Testimonials/ Shout Outs						
	CONVERSION	DM people who viewed, liked, commented, or followed						
		Direct invite to service, experience, or product						
		Follow Ups						
	CUSTOMER SERVICE	Ask for Referrals						
		Engage with Current Clients						
		Answer Emails & Messages						
		Business Development						
		Personal Development						

WEEKLY SOCIAL MEDIA PLAN

THINGS TO CONSIDER

- Captions/Taglines
- Content I Like
- Hashtags
- Objections
- Collaborations
- Pain Points
- Well Received
  Content to Refurbish
- CTA's
- CTT's
- Quotables
- Community Driven
  Content
- Upcoming Events

CONTENT CREATION CHECKLIST

- [ ] Why are you creating this piece of content?

- [ ] Bold Tagline

- [ ] Personal connection/story

- [ ] Call to Think or Call to Act

- [ ] Image (eye-catching and matches the story)

MONDAY	TUESDAY	WEDNESDAY
f FACEBOOK	f	f
⃝ INSTAGRAM	⃝	⃝
⊕ IG STORIES	⊕	⊕

THURSDAY	FRIDAY	SATURDAY	SUNDAY
f	f	f	f
◉	◉	◉	◉
⊕	⊕	⊕	⊕

REFLECT & REFINE

f

POST REACH ∧∨ _____

CURRENT # OF FOLLOWERS ∧∨ _____

MOST ENGAGING POST _____

_____

_____

SHARED / ORIGINAL (CIRCLE ONE)

○ (Instagram)

ACCOUNTS REACHED ∧∨ _____

NEW FOLLOWERS _____

CURRENT FOLLOWERS _____

HIGHEST POST REACH:

_____

MOST SAVED CONTENT _____

MOST SHARED CONTENT _____

OF COLLABORATIONS _____

MOST STORY VIEWS _____

BUSINESS RESULTS

OF INVITES SENT? _____

OF CUSTOMERS ENROLLED? _____

INCOME I EARNED? _____

WEEK ENDING

 👍 WIN > 🌪 PLOT TWIST

♡ WHY (SELF EVALUATION)

◎ BIZ GOALS FOR THE WEEK

4 HASH METHOD

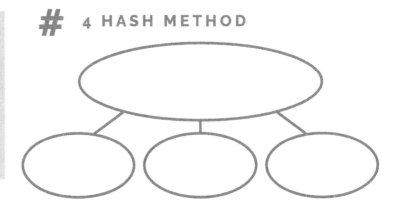

MY INCOME PRODUCING
ACTIVITY TRACKER

WEEK OF _____

			Mon	Tues	Weds	Thur	Fri	Sat	Sun
INCOME PRODUCING ACTIVITIES	**COMMUNITY**	Add Followers							
		Intentional Connect with Followers *not an invite							
		Social Media Post (4 Hash Method)							
		7-10 Stories							
		Highlight People: Testimonials/ Shout Outs							
	CONVERSION	DM people who viewed, liked, commented, or followed							
		Direct invite to service, experience, or product							
		Follow Ups							
	CUSTOMER SERVICE	Ask for Referrals							
		Engage with Current Clients							
		Answer Emails & Messages							
		Business Development							
		Personal Development							

WEEKLY SOCIAL MEDIA PLAN

THINGS TO CONSIDER

- Captions/Taglines
- Content I Like
- Hashtags
- Objections
- Collaborations
- Pain Points
- Well Received
  Content to Refurbish
- CTA's
- CTT's
- Quotables
- Community Driven
  Content
- Upcoming Events

CONTENT CREATION CHECKLIST

- ☐ Why are you creating this piece of content?
- ☐ Bold Tagline
- ☐ Personal connection/story
- ☐ Call to Think or Call to Act
- ☐ Image (eye-catching and matches the story)

MONDAY	TUESDAY	WEDNESDAY
f FACEBOOK	**f**	**f**
⊙ INSTAGRAM	⊙	⊙
⊕ IG STORIES	⊕	⊕

MY GOAL THIS WEEK:

THURSDAY	FRIDAY	SATURDAY	SUNDAY
f	f	f	f
◎	◎	◎	◎
⊕	⊕	⊕	⊕

REFLECT & REFINE

f

POST REACH ∧∨ _____

CURRENT # OF FOLLOWERS ∧∨ _____

MOST ENGAGING POST _____

_____

_____

SHARED / ORIGINAL (CIRCLE ONE)

ACCOUNTS REACHED ∧∨ _____

NEW FOLLOWERS _____

CURRENT FOLLOWERS _____

HIGHEST POST REACH:

_____

MOST SAVED CONTENT _____

MOST SHARED CONTENT _____

OF COLLABORATIONS _____

MOST STORY VIEWS _____

BUSINESS RESULTS

OF INVITES SENT? _____

OF CUSTOMERS ENROLLED? _____

INCOME I EARNED? _____

WEEK ENDING

👍 WIN > 🌪 PLOT TWIST

♡ WHY (SELF EVALUATION)

🎯 BIZ GOALS FOR THE WEEK

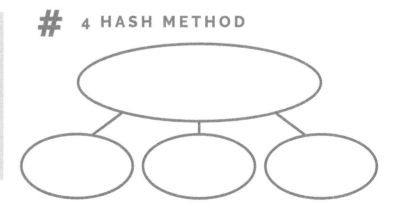

\# 4 HASH METHOD

MY INCOME PRODUCING
ACTIVITY TRACKER

			Mon	Tues	Weds	Thur	Fri	Sat	Sun
INCOME PRODUCING ACTIVITIES	**COMMUNITY**	Add Followers							
		Intentional Connect with Followers *not an invite							
		Social Media Post (4 Hash Method)							
		7-10 Stories							
		Highlight People: Testimonials/ Shout Outs							
	CONVERSION	DM people who viewed, liked, com-mented, or followed							
		Direct invite to service, experience, or product							
		Follow Ups							
	CUSTOMER SERVICE	Ask for Referrals							
		Engage with Current Clients							
		Answer Emails & Messages							
		Business Development							
		Personal Development							

WEEKLY SOCIAL MEDIA PLAN

THINGS TO CONSIDER

- Captions/Taglines
- Content I Like
- Hashtags
- Objections
- Collaborations
- Pain Points
- Well Received Content to Refurbish
- CTA's
- CTT's
- Quotables
- Community Driven Content
- Upcoming Events

CONTENT CREATION CHECKLIST

- ☐ Why are you creating this piece of content?
- ☐ Bold Tagline
- ☐ Personal connection/story
- ☐ Call to Think or Call to Act
- ☐ Image (eye-catching and matches the story)

MONDAY	TUESDAY	WEDNESDAY
f FACEBOOK	**f**	**f**
⦿ INSTAGRAM	⦿	⦿
⊕ IG STORIES	⊕	⊕

THURSDAY	FRIDAY	SATURDAY	SUNDAY
f	f	f	f
⊙	⊙	⊙	⊙
⊕	⊕	⊕	⊕

REFLECT & REFINE

f

POST REACH ^v _____

CURRENT # OF FOLLOWERS ^v _____

MOST ENGAGING POST _____

_____

_____

SHARED / ORIGINAL (CIRCLE ONE)

ⓘ Instagram

ACCOUNTS REACHED ^v _____

NEW FOLLOWERS _____

CURRENT FOLLOWERS _____

HIGHEST POST REACH:

_____

MOST SAVED CONTENT _____

MOST SHARED CONTENT _____

OF COLLABORATIONS _____

MOST STORY VIEWS _____

BUSINESS RESULTS

OF INVITES SENT? _____

OF CUSTOMERS ENROLLED? _____

INCOME I EARNED? _____

WEEK ENDING

👍 WIN > 🌪 PLOT TWIST

♡ WHY (SELF EVALUATION)

🎯 BIZ GOALS FOR THE WEEK

4 HASH METHOD

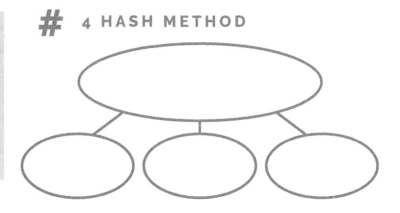

MY INCOME PRODUCING
ACTIVITY TRACKER

			Mon	Tues	Weds	Thur	Fri	Sat	Sun
INCOME PRODUCING ACTIVITIES	**COMMUNITY**	Add Followers							
		Intentional Connect with Followers *not an invite							
		Social Media Post (4 Hash Method)							
		7-10 Stories							
		Highlight People: Testimonials/ Shout Outs							
	CONVERSION	DM people who viewed, liked, commented, or followed							
		Direct invite to service, experience, or product							
		Follow Ups							
	CUSTOMER SERVICE	Ask for Referrals							
		Engage with Current Clients							
		Answer Emails & Messages							
		Business Development							
		Personal Development							

WEEKLY SOCIAL MEDIA PLAN

THINGS TO CONSIDER

- Captions/Taglines
- Content I Like
- Hashtags
- Objections
- Collaborations
- Pain Points
- Well Received Content to Refurbish
- CTA's
- CTT's
- Quotables
- Community Driven Content
- Upcoming Events

CONTENT CREATION CHECKLIST

- ☐ Why are you creating this piece of content?
- ☐ Bold Tagline
- ☐ Personal connection/story
- ☐ Call to Think or Call to Act
- ☐ Image (eye-catching and matches the story)

MONDAY	TUESDAY	WEDNESDAY
f FACEBOOK	f	f
◎ INSTAGRAM	◎	◎
⊕ IG STORIES	⊕	⊕

THURSDAY	FRIDAY	SATURDAY	SUNDAY
f	f	f	f
ⓞ	ⓞ	ⓞ	ⓞ
⊕	⊕	⊕	⊕

month:

_____

marketing focus:

_____
_____
_____
_____
_____
_____
_____
_____
_____
_____
_____
_____

MONDAY	TUESDAY	WEDNESDAY

MONTHLY GOALS:

THURSDAY	FRIDAY	SATURDAY	SUNDAY

REFLECT & REFINE

f

POST REACH ∧∨ _____

CURRENT # OF FOLLOWERS ∧∨ _____

MOST ENGAGING POST _____

_____

_____

SHARED / ORIGINAL (CIRCLE ONE)

📷

ACCOUNTS REACHED ∧∨ _____

NEW FOLLOWERS _____

CURRENT FOLLOWERS _____

HIGHEST POST REACH:

_____

MOST SAVED CONTENT _____

MOST SHARED CONTENT _____

OF COLLABORATIONS _____

MOST STORY VIEWS _____

BUSINESS RESULTS

OF INVITES SENT? _____

OF CUSTOMERS ENROLLED? _____

INCOME I EARNED? _____

WEEK ENDING _____

👍 WIN > 🌪 PLOT TWIST

♡ WHY (SELF EVALUATION)

🎯 BIZ GOALS FOR THE WEEK

4 HASH METHOD

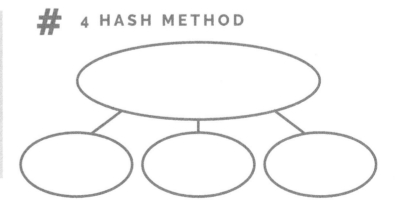

MY INCOME PRODUCING ACTIVITY TRACKER

		Mon	Tues	Weds	Thur	Fri	Sat	Sun
INCOME PRODUCING ACTIVITIES	**COMMUNITY**							
		Add Followers						
		Intentional Connect with Followers *not an invite						
		Social Media Post (4 Hash Method)						
		7-10 Stories						
		Highlight People: Testimonials/ Shout Outs						
	CONVERSION	DM people who viewed, liked, commented, or followed						
		Direct invite to service, experience, or product						
		Follow Ups						
	CUSTOMER SERVICE	Ask for Referrals						
		Engage with Current Clients						
		Answer Emails & Messages						
		Business Development						
		Personal Development						

WEEKLY SOCIAL MEDIA PLAN

THINGS TO CONSIDER

- Captions/Taglines
- Content I Like
- Hashtags
- Objections
- Collaborations
- Pain Points
- Well Received
  Content to Refurbish
- CTA's
- CTT's
- Quotables
- Community Driven
  Content
- Upcoming Events

CONTENT CREATION CHECKLIST

- ☐ Why are you
  creating this
  piece of content?

- ☐ Bold Tagline

- ☐ Personal
  connection/story

- ☐ Call to Think or
  Call to Act

- ☐ Image (eye-
  catching and
  matches the
  story)

	MONDAY	TUESDAY	WEDNESDAY
f FACEBOOK	**f**	**f**	
◎ INSTAGRAM	◎	◎	
⊕ IG STORIES	⊕	⊕	

THURSDAY	FRIDAY	SATURDAY	SUNDAY
f	f	f	f
ⓞ	ⓞ	ⓞ	ⓞ
⊕	⊕	⊕	⊕

REFLECT & REFINE

f

POST REACH ^∨ _____

CURRENT # OF FOLLOWERS ^∨ _____

MOST ENGAGING POST _____

_____

_____

SHARED / ORIGINAL (CIRCLE ONE)

Instagram

ACCOUNTS REACHED ^∨ _____

NEW FOLLOWERS _____

CURRENT FOLLOWERS _____

HIGHEST POST REACH:

_____

MOST SAVED CONTENT _____

MOST SHARED CONTENT _____

OF COLLABORATIONS _____

MOST STORY VIEWS _____

BUSINESS RESULTS

OF INVITES SENT? _____

OF CUSTOMERS ENROLLED? _____

INCOME I EARNED? _____

WEEK ENDING

👍 WIN > 🌪 PLOT TWIST

♡ WHY (SELF EVALUATION)

◎ BIZ GOALS FOR THE WEEK

4 HASH METHOD

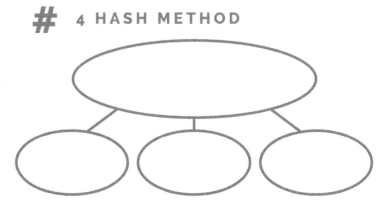

MY INCOME PRODUCING
ACTIVITY TRACKER

WEEK OF

		Mon	Tues	Weds	Thur	Fri	Sat	Sun
INCOME PRODUCING ACTIVITIES	**COMMUNITY**	Add Followers						
		Intentional Connect with Followers *not an invite						
		Social Media Post (4 Hash Method)						
		7-10 Stories						
		Highlight People: Testimonials/ Shout Outs						
	CONVERSION	DM people who viewed, liked, commented, or followed						
		Direct invite to service, experience, or product						
		Follow Ups						
	CUSTOMER SERVICE	Ask for Referrals						
		Engage with Current Clients						
		Answer Emails & Messages						
		Business Development						
		Personal Development						

WEEKLY SOCIAL MEDIA PLAN

THINGS TO CONSIDER

- Captions/Taglines
- Content I Like
- Hashtags
- Objections
- Collaborations
- Pain Points
- Well Received Content to Refurbish
- CTA's
- CTT's
- Quotables
- Community Driven Content
- Upcoming Events

CONTENT CREATION CHECKLIST

- [ ] Why are you creating this piece of content?
- [ ] Bold Tagline
- [ ] Personal connection/story
- [ ] Call to Think or Call to Act
- [ ] Image (eye-catching and matches the story)

MONDAY	TUESDAY	WEDNESDAY
f FACEBOOK	f	f
⊙ INSTAGRAM	⊙	⊙
⊕ IG STORIES	⊕	⊕

THURSDAY	FRIDAY	SATURDAY	SUNDAY
f	f	f	f
ⓘ	ⓘ	ⓘ	ⓘ
⊕	⊕	⊕	⊕

REFLECT & REFINE

f

POST REACH ˄˅ _____

CURRENT # OF FOLLOWERS ˄˅ _____

MOST ENGAGING POST _____

_____

_____

SHARED / ORIGINAL (CIRCLE ONE)

⌾

ACCOUNTS REACHED ˄˅ _____

NEW FOLLOWERS _____

CURRENT FOLLOWERS _____

HIGHEST POST REACH:

_____

MOST SAVED CONTENT _____

MOST SHARED CONTENT _____

OF COLLABORATIONS _____

MOST STORY VIEWS _____

BUSINESS RESULTS

OF INVITES SENT? _____

OF CUSTOMERS ENROLLED? _____

INCOME I EARNED? _____

WEEK ENDING

👍 WIN > 🌪 PLOT TWIST

 WHY (SELF EVALUATION)

🎯 BIZ GOALS FOR THE WEEK

4 HASH METHOD

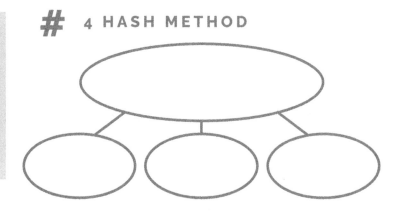

MY INCOME PRODUCING
ACTIVITY TRACKER

		Mon	Tues	Weds	Thur	Fri	Sat	Sun
INCOME PRODUCING ACTIVITIES	**COMMUNITY**	Add Followers						
		Intentional Connect with Followers *not an invite						
		Social Media Post (4 Hash Method)						
		7-10 Stories						
		Highlight People: Testimonials/ Shout Outs						
	CONVERSION	DM people who viewed, liked, com- mented, or followed						
		Direct invite to service, experience, or product						
		Follow Ups						
	CUSTOMER SERVICE	Ask for Referrals						
		Engage with Current Clients						
		Answer Emails & Messages						
		Business Development						
		Personal Development						

WEEKLY SOCIAL MEDIA PLAN

THINGS TO CONSIDER

- Captions/Taglines
- Content I Like
- Hashtags
- Objections
- Collaborations
- Pain Points
- Well Received Content to Refurbish
- CTA's
- CTT's
- Quotables
- Community Driven Content
- Upcoming Events

CONTENT CREATION CHECKLIST

- ☐ Why are you creating this piece of content?
- ☐ Bold Tagline
- ☐ Personal connection/story
- ☐ Call to Think or Call to Act
- ☐ Image (eye-catching and matches the story)

MONDAY	TUESDAY	WEDNESDAY
f FACEBOOK	**f**	**f**
⃝ INSTAGRAM	⃝	⃝
⊕ IG STORIES	⊕	⊕

MY GOAL THIS WEEK:

THURSDAY	FRIDAY	SATURDAY	SUNDAY
f	f	f	f
⊙	⊙	⊙	⊙
⊕	⊕	⊕	⊕

REFLECT & REFINE

f

POST REACH ∧∨ _____

CURRENT # OF FOLLOWERS ∧∨ _____

MOST ENGAGING POST _____

_____

_____

SHARED / ORIGINAL (CIRCLE ONE)

📷

ACCOUNTS REACHED ∧∨ _____

NEW FOLLOWERS _____

CURRENT FOLLOWERS _____

HIGHEST POST REACH:

_____

MOST SAVED CONTENT _____

MOST SHARED CONTENT _____

OF COLLABORATIONS _____

MOST STORY VIEWS _____

BUSINESS RESULTS

OF INVITES SENT? _____

OF CUSTOMERS ENROLLED? _____

INCOME I EARNED? _____

 👍 WIN > 🌪 PLOT TWIST

♡ WHY (SELF EVALUATION)

◎ BIZ GOALS FOR THE WEEK

4 HASH METHOD

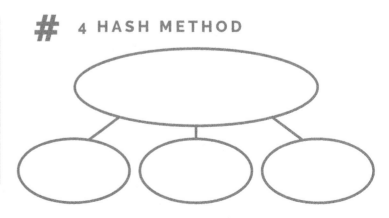

MY INCOME PRODUCING ACTIVITY TRACKER

		Mon	Tues	Weds	Thur	Fri	Sat	Sun
INCOME PRODUCING ACTIVITIES	**COMMUNITY** — Add Followers							
	Intentional Connect with Followers *not an invite							
	Social Media Post (4 Hash Method)							
	7-10 Stories							
	Highlight People: Testimonials/ Shout Outs							
	CONVERSION — DM people who viewed, liked, commented, or followed							
	Direct invite to service, experience, or product							
	Follow Ups							
	CUSTOMER SERVICE — Ask for Referrals							
	Engage with Current Clients							
	Answer Emails & Messages							
	Business Development							
	Personal Development							

WEEKLY SOCIAL MEDIA PLAN

THINGS TO CONSIDER

- Captions/Taglines
- Content I Like
- Hashtags
- Objections
- Collaborations
- Pain Points
- Well Received Content to Refurbish
- CTA's
- CTT's
- Quotables
- Community Driven Content
- Upcoming Events

CONTENT CREATION CHECKLIST

- ☐ Why are you creating this piece of content?
- ☐ Bold Tagline
- ☐ Personal connection/story
- ☐ Call to Think or Call to Act
- ☐ Image (eye-catching and matches the story)

MONDAY	TUESDAY	WEDNESDAY
f FACEBOOK	f	f
⊙ INSTAGRAM	⊙	⊙
⊕ IG STORIES	⊕	⊕

THURSDAY	FRIDAY	SATURDAY	SUNDAY
f	f	f	f
◙	◙	◙	◙
⊕	⊕	⊕	⊕

REFLECT & REFINE

f

POST REACH ∧∨ _____

CURRENT # OF FOLLOWERS ∧∨ _____

MOST ENGAGING POST _____

_____

_____

SHARED / ORIGINAL (CIRCLE ONE)

(Instagram)

ACCOUNTS REACHED ∧∨ _____

NEW FOLLOWERS _____

CURRENT FOLLOWERS _____

HIGHEST POST REACH:

_____

MOST SAVED CONTENT _____

MOST SHARED CONTENT _____

OF COLLABORATIONS _____

MOST STORY VIEWS _____

BUSINESS RESULTS

OF INVITES SENT? _____

OF CUSTOMERS ENROLLED? _____

INCOME I EARNED? _____

WEEK ENDING

👍 WIN > 🌪 PLOT TWIST

♡ WHY (SELF EVALUATION)

🎯 BIZ GOALS FOR THE WEEK

4 HASH METHOD

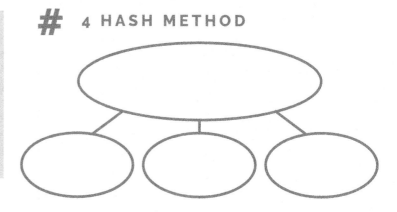

MY INCOME PRODUCING ACTIVITY TRACKER

		Mon	Tues	Weds	Thur	Fri	Sat	Sun
INCOME PRODUCING ACTIVITIES	**COMMUNITY**	Add Followers							
		Intentional Connect with Followers *not an invite							
		Social Media Post (4 Hash Method)							
		7-10 Stories							
		Highlight People: Testimonials/ Shout Outs							
	CONVERSION	DM people who viewed, liked, commented, or followed							
		Direct invite to service, experience, or product							
		Follow Ups							
	CUSTOMER SERVICE	Ask for Referrals							
		Engage with Current Clients							
		Answer Emails & Messages							
		Business Development							
		Personal Development							

WEEKLY SOCIAL MEDIA PLAN

THINGS TO CONSIDER

- Captions/Taglines
- Content I Like
- Hashtags
- Objections
- Collaborations
- Pain Points
- Well Received Content to Refurbish
- CTA's
- CTT's
- Quotables
- Community Driven Content
- Upcoming Events

CONTENT CREATION CHECKLIST

- ☐ Why are you creating this piece of content?
- ☐ Bold Tagline
- ☐ Personal connection/story
- ☐ Call to Think or Call to Act
- ☐ Image (eye-catching and matches the story)

MONDAY	TUESDAY	WEDNESDAY
f FACEBOOK	**f**	**f**
ⓞ INSTAGRAM	ⓞ	ⓞ
⊕ IG STORIES	⊕	⊕

MY GOAL THIS WEEK:

THURSDAY	FRIDAY	SATURDAY	SUNDAY
f	f	f	f
⊙	⊙	⊙	⊙
⊕	⊕	⊕	⊕

WELCOME TO THE 1% CLUB, FRIEND.

You did it!!! You are here at the end of the planner which means you have planned and executed a full years' worth of social media content. I know without a doubt that you have learned so much through this experience, how could you not? Experience is always the best teacher. You have learned so much about your brand, your voice, and what truly brings you joy in what you do. We have no doubt that the more you continue to plan and create content you are going to continue to reach and impact more people.

As experts in the field of online business, we know firsthand how challenging it can be to navigate the ever changing trends of social media. But you are doing the dang thing and so are we. In January of 2019, we launched "Chic Influencer" while still growing our network marketing businesses. There were so many new challenges and hurdles to navigate. We completely understand what it is like to follow your passion in the midst of creating something new. Every single day we were faced with obstacles that required us to fail our way forward and truly live from a place of "figuring it out".

You guys, we do not have ALL the answers. But we refuse to NOT FIGURE IT OUT. We know it's not about one perfect post. It's about the consistent act of showing up daily, serving your audience, and creating momentum that **#makeschichappen**.

We believe in you, we hope you know our mission is to help you bridge the gap from where you are now to where you are called to go. We are rooting for you, and we are in the trenches along side of you every single day.

Your sisters in chic,

Melanie Mitro   *Katy Ursta*

CHICINFLUENCER.COM

Share your Make Chic Happen Plans with us on
social media by tagging us @chicinfluencer
Tell us how your planner is changing your business strategy.

To get more tips from us you can also subscribe
to the **Make Chic Happen podcast** on iTunes, Spotify,
Soundcloud, or anywhere you can download podcasts.

ACKNOWLEDGEMENTS

So much love to our families for supporting us with our BIG idea, especially our husbands (Matt and Mike) who see first hand the good, the bad, and all the mess that goes into growing a business.

We are forever grateful for our Chic Influencer community with whom we have the honor of being in the entrepreneurial trenches with everyday. You make us better.

To Alysa Gumto, Kate Speer, and Molly Corrigan, our partners in Chic. Thanks for keeping our marbles in the jar. Chic doesn't happen without you, our #kajabiqueen and #media-moguls. Thanks for all you do behind the scenes.

To Margaret Cogswell, who helped us take this BIG idea and messy first draft and turn it into what it is now, the **#makechichappen** planner.

Lastly, you, our friend, busy building your business at the kitchen table, in the car, or on the couch cuddled up with your laptop. Thank you for letting us be a part of your journey. Always rooting for you.

xoxo.

Melanie and Katy

Made in the USA
Coppell, TX
19 December 2020